Police-Community
Relations

Prentice-Hall
Essentials of Law Enforcement Series

James D. Stinchcomb
Series Editor

Police-Community Relations

ALAN COFFEY

EDWARD ELDEFONSO

WALTER HARTINGER

PRENTICE-HALL, INC.
Englewood Cliffs, N.J.

P 13–684605–X
C 13–684613–O
Library of Congress Catalog Card Number: 79–143031
Printed in the United States of America

Current printing (last digit):
10   9   8   7   6   5   4   3   2   1

PRENTICE-HALL INTERNATIONAL, INC., *London*
PRENTICE-HALL OF AUSTRALIA PTY. LTD., *Sydney*
PRENTICE-HALL OF CANADA LTD., *Toronto*
PRENTICE-HALL OF INDIA PRIVATE LIMITED, *New Delhi*
PRENTICE-HALL OF JAPAN, INC., *Tokyo*

Introduction

Surely nothing can be more fundamental to guaranteeing the delivery of professional services than the employment of properly trained personnel. In pursuit of that goal, law enforcement officers and those who train them have long recognized the need for concise yet thoroughly documented information, well-researched and accurately presented.

In recent years, several commendable efforts have resulted in the availability of some valuable training resources. But too few of these were professionally developed by the textbook publishing companies, although their assistance was becoming imperative. The Prentice-Hall Essentials of Law Enforcement Series has been developed following a conference of national authorities who were asked to determine topics for priority production. The subject areas chosen are both timely and critical to the police and to their own increased determination to improve their service.

The potential use for this series is limited only by the creative imaginations of those responsible for peace officers' access to learning. Each book may perform as a supplement to a college course, as a resource for a training program, or as a reader to encourage informal study. It is the hope and the intent of the publisher, the editor, and the authors that these practical texts will contribute to the continuing progress being achieved by the nation's police.

James D. Stinchcomb

Institute for Justice
and Law Enforcement
Washington, D.C.

Statement of Purpose

The California Commission on Peace Officers Standards and Training (POST), formed by the California legislation in 1959 to upgrade the training of peace officers, stated: "In some urban areas, the police and the community seem to stand in conflict which interferes seriously with public confidence in the police, and consequently, with the ability of the police to deal effectively with the crime problem." Without doubt, the public's hostility toward and lack of confidence in the police, interfere with police recruiting, morale, day-to-day police operations, and safety of the individual officer, and, in general, have an adverse effect on "total community stability." Because a police department's capacity to deal with crime depends to a large extent on its relationship with the citizenry, no lasting improvement in law enforcement is likely unless police-community relations are substantially improved.

Government officials, criminologists, political scientists, doctors, police officials, and many other competent citizens are of the opinion that with a steadily increasing emphasis on constitutional rights, the law enforcement methods used to anticipate and prevent disturbance must shift in emphasis toward community relations and human relations programs. The relatively uncomplicated function of dealing with traditional crime may well prove one of the policeman's lesser responsibilities as the tensions mount between various segments of the population.

There is nothing new about law enforcement's seeking to anticipate and prevent violation of law or the disturbance of peace. Nor is there anything new about deliberate efforts to keep the public informed about law enforcement. What *is* new, however, is the concept of law enforcement being *actively* involved in programs to reduce general community tensions.

The purpose of this text is to provide a resource in training police in the complexity of community and human relations.

Law enforcement is now unquestionably faced with an

unprecedented urgency in developing line officers capable not only of enforcing law but also of participating in the resolution of the social problems that create much of the crime.

This text approaches social problems from the point of view that police are primarily responsible for enforcing law and only indirectly responsible for the resolution of social problems. But out of deference to the courage and dignity with which police have confronted the enormous social unrest of this era, this text seeks to isolate the nature and scope of police-community relations.

Acknowledgments

With the usual proviso that they cannot be held accountable for either errors of omission or commission, the authors express their gratitude for the advise, counsel, and encouragement tendered by B. Earl Lewis, Director of the Department of Law Enforcement Education, De Anza College, Ben W. Lashkoff, Inspector, intelligence unit, San Francisco Police Department (for providing photographs and other illustrations), Robert E. Nino, Chief Juvenile Probation Officer, Santa Clara County Juvenile Probation Department, and his assistants—Richard Bothman and Michael Kuzarian. Also we wish to thank David Lagassé, Supervising Probation Officer (and special friend), and Nelson A. Watson, International Association of Chiefs of Police.

Finally, we are grateful to our wives, Beverly May Coffey, Mildred Ann Eldefonso, and Patricia Hartinger and our children for being patient and supportive while we spent most of our "spare" time on this enterprise.

Alan Coffey
Edward Eldefonso
Walter Hartinger

Contents

Police-Community Relations

Introduction to the Problem of Police image in a Changing Community

Law enforcement and the equal administration of justice have become major national concerns in recent years. The rapid growth of our cities—with attendant problems in housing, education, employment, and social welfare services—has accentuated these concerns and has been highlighted by the increasing urban concentration of minority groups.

Crime rates have generally been higher in these areas where poverty, family disintegration, unemployment, lack of education, minority group frustration, and resentment in the face of social and economic discrimination—the ghetto syndrome—are manifest. The expectations, excitements, and additional frustrations engendered by the civil rights movement have compounded the difficulties in law enforcement and the administration of justice.

Foremost among these difficulties are the relationships among police, minority groups, and the general community. There is increasing evidence of deterioration in these relationships, particularly between police and Blacks. There are widespread charges of "police brutality" and demands for greater assertion of civilian control over police actions. On the other hand, many police officials decry the growing disrespect for law, public apathy, molly-coddling of "criminals" by the courts, and political influence on the law enforcement process. Some police continue to view civil rights groups as trouble makers, disruptive of the law and order the police have sworn to uphold, while at the same time, some Blacks and Puerto Ricans hold a stereotyped image of the policeman. These misconceptions severely hamper cooperative relationships.

A presidential commission (The National Advisory Commission on Civil Disorders) reported recently that many Negroes may "come to support not only riots but . . . rebellion," unless multibillion dollar measures are taken quickly to try to heal racial bitterness and riot ravages in city slums.

chapter

1

The *National Advisory Commission on Civil Disorders*, named to investigate street riots, stated in harsh, vivid detail that:

> The police are not merely a "spark" factor. To some Negroes, police have come to symbolize white power, white racism and white repression. And, the fact is that many police do reflect and express these white attitudes. The atmosphere of hostility and cynicism is reinforced by a widespread belief among Negroes in the existence of police brutality and a "double standard" of justice and protection —one for Negroes and one for whites.

Although the situation confronting the law enforcement officer in the United States is less than ideal, he is still responsible for the maintenance of an orderly American society through law. Of course, laws of the United States continue to include the minimum obligations imposed on any free

Fig. 1.1 An important obligation or police responsibility is the protection of property. Quite often this particular responsibility is not accorded its due priority by groups of individuals who stress individual "rights and freedom." Photo courtesy of the San Francisco Police Department.

The Problem of Police Image in a Changing Community

society by those who have observed the law: To provide in an *impartial manner* both *personal safety* and *property security*. In this fundamental context, all regulated behavior—from family activities to vehicle speed—is a law enforcement function.

As the complexities of maintaining order multiply, an ever-increasing responsibility must shift to those who enforce the law. This responsibility is to anticipate and to *prevent* disruption (of any kind) of an orderly society.

Police Power

Law must be enforced if civilized man is to survive. Society cannot depend completely on simple persuasion to induce law observance, and therefore it must require enforcement of law. The term *enforcement* implies, as does the very nature of man, the potential use of force, and this potential, then, is necessarily a part of the police role. But the manner in which this potential is viewed by the public often determines whether the police image is good or bad. Because good police image tends, to affect favorably an individual's willingness to observe the law voluntarily, police retain a rightful interest in a good image. The law enforcement officer embodies the law so visibly and directly that neither the policemen nor the public find it easy to differentiate between the law and its enforcement. As B. Smith pointed out:

> Relatively few citizens recall ever having seen a judge; fewer still, a prosecutor, coroner, sheriff, probation officer or prison warden. The patrolman is thoroughly familiar to all. His uniform picks him out from the crowd so distinctly that he becomes a living symbol of the law—not always of its majesty, but certainly of its power. Whether the police like it or not, they are forever marked men.[1]

Because any officer of the law is partly a symbol, law enforcement work consists to some extent of creating illusions. Thus, a police vehicle can slow down turnpike traffic or "motivate" drivers to make stops at designated intersec-

[1]B. Smith, "Municipal Police Administration," *Annals of the American Academy of Police and Social Science*, Vol. 40, No. 5, p. 22.

Police Power

Fig. 1.2 The *potential* to wield force is a necessary part of police work. How this "force" is utilized, the professional manner in which it is carried out determines whether the response will be positive or negative. Photo courtesy of the San Francisco Police Department.

tions, and the presence of a half-dozen officers can control a large crowd.[2]

A realistic appraisal of civil disturbances in our society necessarily results in awareness that the struggle and operation of a democratic society contain inherent violence-producing factors. The identification and labeling of these factors should not be interpreted as criticism of either the society or its philo-

[2]H. H. Toch, "Psychological Consequences of the Police Role," *Police*, Vol. 10, No. 1, September-October, 1965, 22.

The Problem of Police Image in a Changing Community

sophical basis, but rather as a reasonable attempt to define the *nature* of the problem.

Society must be made aware of the attainable goals of law enforcement *before* programs are devised that seek either total elimination of destructive riots and civil disobedience or —conversely—a feeling of total inability to increase protection of our society. Therefore, it is important to point out that the *degree* of police power required for the provision of a society free from chaotic racial disorders would be enough to destroy all pretense of individual liberty. Similarly, the rejecttion of the *concept* that such disorders can be better controlled and reduced would result in *anarchy* (the complete absence of government and law). Law enforcement must continue to strive between these two alternatives, and police power must be carefully used in civil disturbances to avoid its becoming a barrier against long-term changes in the community's social structure.

The Police and the Community

The need for strengthening the relationships of police with the communities they serve is critical. Negroes, Puerto Ricans, Mexican-Americans, Indians, and other minority groups are taking action to acquire rights and services which have been historically denied them. Law enforcement agencies, as the most visible representative of the society from which minority groups are demanding fair treatment and equal opportunity, are faced with unprecedented situations today which require that they develop new policies and practices specifically for dealing with the problems of these groups.

Even if fairer treatment of minority groups were their sole consideration, police departments would have an obligation to attempt to achieve and maintain a positive public image and good police-community relations. In fact, however, much more is at stake. Police-community relationships have a direct bearing on the character of life in the cities and on the community's ability to maintain stability and to solve its problems. At the same time, a police department's capacity to deal with crime depends to a large extent upon its relationship with the citizenry. Indeed, no lasting improvement in law enforcement is likely in this country unless police-community relations are substantially improved.

In a fundamental sense, however, it is wrong to define the problem of the police and the community solely as hostility to police. In many ways, the policeman only symbolizes much deeper problems. Responsibility for apathy or disrespect for law enforcement agencies would be more appropriately attributed to:

> ... a social system that permits inequities and irregularities in law, stimulates poverty and inhibits initiative and motivation of the poor, and regulates low social and economic status to the police while concomitantly giving them more extraneous non-police duties than adequately can be performed.[3]

To a considerable extent, then, the police are the victims of community problems which are not of their making. For generations, minority groups and the poor have not received a fair opportunity to share the benefits of American life. The policeman in the ghetto is the most visible *symbol* of a society from which many ghetto residents (particularly the Negroes) are increasingly alienated.[4]

> At the same time, police responsibilities in the ghetto are greater than elsewhere in the community since the other institutions of social control have so little authority: The schools, because so many are segregated, old and inferior; religion, which has become irrelevant to those who have lost faith as they lost hope; career aspirations, which for many Negroes are totally lacking; the family, because its bonds are so often snapped. It is the policeman who must deal with the consequences of this institutional vacuum and is then resented for the presence and measures this effort demands.[5]

The policeman, furthermore, has unfortunately become a symbol not only of law, but of the entire system of law

---

[3]R. L. Derbyshire, "The Social Control Role of the Police in Changing Urban Communities," *Excerpta Criminologica*, Vol. 6, No. 3, 1966, pp. 315–316.

[4]*The Challenge of Crime in a Free Society*, A Report by the President's Commission on Law Enforcement and Administration of Justice (U.S. Government Printing Office), Wash., D.C., 1967, p. 150; see also, The National Advisory Commission on Civil Disorders, p. 157.

[5]*Ibid.*

The Problem of Police Image in a Changing Community

enforcement and criminal justice. As such, he becomes the tangible target for grievances against shortcomings throughout that system:

> When a suspect is held for long periods in jail prior to trial because he cannot make bail, when he is given inadequate counsel or none at all, when he is assigned counsel that attempts to extract from him or his family even though he is indigent, when he is paraded through the courtroom in a group or is tried in a few minutes, when he is sent to jail because he has no money to pay a fine, when the jail or prison is physically dilapidated or its personnel brutal or incompetent, or when the probation or parole officer has little time to give him, the offender will probably blame, at least in part, the police officers who have arrested him and started the process.[6]

The policeman assigned to the ghetto is a symbol of increasingly bitter social debate over law enforcement. The Commission on Civil Disorders noted that one side, disturbed and perplexed by sharp rises in crime and urban violence, exerts extreme pressure on police for tougher law enforcement. Another group, inflamed against police as agents of repression, tends toward defiance of what it regards as order maintained at the expense of justice.[7]

However, only in Utopia would every citizen feel respect and friendliness toward the police. A certain amount of resentment on the part of the public is natural and must be expected:

> A police force gains the respect for the community it serves by carrying out its functions in a spirit of toleration, human kindness and good will toward all men. This is a difficult task, because people in every community have many standards of morality, and although they are willing to obey some of our laws, they are determined to violate others. Therefore, the policeman is never popular with all classes of persons. He is, of course, looked upon by the vicious and lawless as their natural enemy. He is considered to be an obstructionist by every arrogant and selfish citizen who desires to indulge his own self-seeking whims and inclinations, to the annoyance or the disadvantage of others. He is often and will continue to be used as a foot stool by every

---

[6] Ibid.

[7] Ibid. The National Advisory Commission on Civil Disorders, p. 157.

The Police and the Community

crack-brained reformer whose ideas are born of emotion-alism. And the reputation of the fine, manly, decent men who comprise the overwhelming majority of police organizations will probably continue to be besmirched by the bad conduct of the comparatively few in police organizations who prove false to the trust placed in them.[8]

Policemen, then, must be realistic—they must realize that the people they serve will not universally like or respect them:

Today's policemen are the heirs of that frightful legacy of ill will built up over many years—the man who walks the street bitter at the police may still be harboring a grudge of forty years standing. The policeman who embittered him may long ago have gone to his reward, but his successors must suffer the consequences.[9]

Complaints of Harassment and Brutality as They Affect the Police Image

Professionalization has not made police personnel insensitive to public criticism. Because law enforcement personnel are extremely sensitive to public criticism, identification with fellow officers is reinforced, thereby "forging a social bond among them, at the same time that it generates a great deal of mutual suspicion."[10]

The fact that a policeman must constantly be "on his guard" against physical injury (statistics indicate that there is a definite increase in assaults against policemen), may tend to contribute to his feeling of isolation and to his view of the community as a threat. Such feelings (isolation) tend to increase the possibility of "overreaction" when a policeman is confronted with a threatening situation. His natural reaction is to strike first. This idea of the *symbolic assailant* illustrates one of the two principal variables which make up the working person of a police officer—*reaction to danger*. The other is

[8]J. J. Skehan, *Modern Police Work* (New York: Francis M. Basuino, 1951), pp. 8–9.
[9]E. Adlow, *Policemen and People* (Boston: William J. Rockfort, 1947), p. 17.
[10]D. J. Dodd, "Police Mentality and Behavior," *Issues in Criminology*, University of California, Berkeley, Vol. 3, No. 1, Summer, 1967, pp. 47–67.

The Problem of Police Image in a Changing Community

his *reaction to authority*. His natural suspicion and his conception of his work as a way of life reinforce the tendencies mentioned above and draw him further away from the public he intends to serve and protect.[11]

> ... this is especially so in the lower class areas, where the cop is seen as standing for the interests and prejudices of dominant (white) society in the role of the oppressor, and where each party sees the other as a misfit.[12]

Since a community's attitude toward the police is influenced by the actions of individual officers on the streets, courteous and tolerant behavior by policemen in their contacts with citizens is a must. According to a report by the President's Commission on Law Enforcement and Administration of Justice[13] there have been instances of unambiguous harassment and physical abuse on the part of law enforcement. Nelson A. Watson, Project Supervisor, Research and Development Division, International Association of Chiefs of Police, gave the following report at a police administrators' conference regarding police action:

> So far as police action is concerned, there are things that come to my attention on that, too. I hear of the incidents from police and from civil rights workers. I read about them in the press, in magazines, and books. I cannot vouch for the accuracy of these reports because we all know how easily things can get distorted and misinterpreted. But accurate or not, it is vitally important that we all remember that people form opinions and take action on the basis of what they hear and what they believe without checking its accuracy. Things like the following illustrate what people are saying, what they believe, and what is back of the way they behave:
>
> *Case No. 1*
> "The cops pulled us over and came up to the car with guns in their hands. This one cop (incidentally, the officer was a Negro) told me to show him my license and registration. When I asked him why, he told me to do as I was told and

[11] *Ibid.*
[12] *Ibid.*
[13] *The Challenge of Crime in a Free Society,* A report by the President's Commission on Law Enforcement and Administration of Justice (Wash., D.C.: U.S. Government Printing Office), 1967, p. 102.

The Police and the Community

not get smart. Then they made us all get out of the car while the other guy looked inside. When they couldn't find anything wrong, they told us we could go. I asked them what it was all about and the one cop said they had a lot of stolen cars around there lately so they had to check up."

Case No. 2

A newspaper reported that a man had complained about the actions of an officer which he felt were uncalled for. It was reported the officer had arrested a man and had hand-cuffed him. For some reason, the man fell to the ground and the complainant said the officer then put his foot on the man's neck. The complainant said the arrested man was not fighting the officer, and after all, he was handcuffed. He cited this as an example of police brutality.

Case No. 3

An officer patrolling a beach where kids had caused trouble approached a teenage boy who was sitting by himself on a bench drinking from a bottle. Drinking liquor by minors was forbidden by law. The officer asked the boy what he was drinking and the boy replied that it was Coke. The officer took the bottle and smelled the contents finding that it contained no liquor so that he had no basis for arrest. The officer poured the remainder of the drink onto the sand and ordered the boy to move along.

Case No. 4

With respect to the Puerto Rican disturbances in Chicago recently, the Christian Science Monitor reported as follows: "There was little doubt that the presence of police—and their handling of Puerto Ricans over a period of several years—was the center of the controversy in this conflict. We heard no other argument or issue in the seven hours we worked the streets. . . . Despite careful guidelines, police tactics were not uniformly discreet. One instance took place before we began breaking up the congestion at Division and California. Most of the young men had gone, and we had been thanked by the sergeant on the corner. Suddenly, a police captain with a dozen blue-helmeted men stormed across the street. I was standing inside a restaurant at the time because the street was virtually clear. The captain and three men pushed into the restaurant where more than 50 people, in family groups, were quietly eating their evening meal. In a loud voice, he demanded to see the owner. Moving to the kitchen, he demanded that she clear the place and close up. Then he stalked out, shaking his fist and shouting: 'I'll give you 15 minutes to get everybody out of here, you understand. Fifteen minutes.' Then he slammed the door with such force the storefront windows rattled. In less than a minute, he had changed quietness into anger. . . . A spokesman for the police department said it was only one of several complaints about the same captain. At 10:50 p.m., only a handful of people were left on the street. A lieutenant and a group of policemen raced to the upper floor of a three-story building on Division Street and hauled out two men who someone said had been seen with crude anti-police signs in a window. Then the police closed a restaurant below where there were a number of young Puerto Ricans. Those in the restaurant scattered as ordered. But two youths, walking slowly a block away were spotted by a sergeant who cursed them, saying to the lieutenant: 'Those guys were in the restaurant. Let's go get them.' At this point, the only incident of undue physical roughness I observed during the entire night took place. Two police searched one of the youths, and then gave him a hard shove that sent him sprawling toward the police wagon. The lieutenant and sergeant stood on the curb discussing what they could charge the two youths with since they had only been walking down the street. . . ."

Watson concluded this portion of his address to the conference by stating:

Now, as I said, I cannot vouch for the accuracy of these reports. I suspect there is a considerable bias in them. I also realize that when they are shaved down in the retelling, there may be significant facts omitted. *But the point is that these are the kinds of things people hear, and it is on the basis of such stories they form their opinions about police.** Then, when approached by an officer they expect rough, inconsiderate, impolite treatment.

I know and so do you that it sometimes takes pretty strong talk and forceful action to get the police job done. However, I am sure we can agree that an officer who uses profanity is definitely out of line. So is one who is so prejudiced that he cannot treat the objects of his prejudice as ordinary human beings. An officer who generates resentment, who makes people rise up in anger by the things he says or does or the way he acts toward them is a source of trouble. An officer who would stand by and watch someone being beaten is violating his oath. One of the things that we must attend to in our effort to improve relations with the people in our communities, therefore, is the way our officers are doing

*Italics supplied by authors.

The Police and the Community

their job on the street day in and day out. This is not to say that *all* the fault lies in police behavior, but, to the extent that *any* of the fault lies there, we must accept the blame and correct it.[14]

The President's Commission observed that physical abuse is only one source of aggravation in the ghetto. In nearly every city surveyed, the Commission heard complaints of harassment of interracial couples, dispersal of social street gatherings, and the stopping of Negroes on foot or in cars without objective basis. These, together with contemptuous and degrading verbal abuse, have great impact in the ghetto —impact on attitudes toward law enforcement personnel. Such conduct, relates the Commission, strips the Negro of the one thing he may have left—his dignity, "the question of being a man."

"Harassment" or discourtesy, according to the President's Commission, may not be the result of malicious or discriminatory intent of police officers. Many officers simply fail to understand the effects of their actions because of their limited knowledge of the Negro community. Calling a Negro teenager by his first name may instill resentment, because many whites still refuse to extend to adult Negroes the courtesy of the title "Mister." A patrolman may take the arm of a person he is leading to the police car. Negroes are more likely to resent this than whites because the action implies that they are on the verge of flight and may degrade them in the eyes of friends or onlookers.[15]

The Commission observers also have found that most officers handle their rigorous work with considerable coolness. They have found that there is no pronounced racial pattern in the kind of behavior just described. The tendency is for officers to treat blue-collar citizens, regardless of race, in such a fashion. However, all such behavior is obviously and totally reprehensible, and when it is directed against minority-group citizens, it is particularly likely to lead to bitterness in the community. The fact that provocation and physical danger do exist does not excuse an intolerant de-

[14]N. A. Watson, "The Fringes of Police-Community Relations," *Police Administrators' Conference, Indiana University Medical Center, Indianapolis, Indiana,* International Association of Chiefs of Police, Washington, D.C., June 29, 1966.

[15]*The Challenge of Crime in a Free Society,* A report by the President's Commission, p. 102.

The Problem of Police Image in a Changing Community

Fig. 1.3 There is no doubt that under stressful situations there may be occasions in which attempts will be made to provoke over-reaction on the part of law enforcement officers. When action—such as making an arrest—is dictated, coolness and a professional approach must be maintained. Photo courtesy of the San Francisco Police Department.

meanor on the part of police officers.[16] O. W. Wilson, recently retired Chicago police superintendent and distinguished author of numerous law enforcement textbooks, stated:[17]

> The officer must remember that there is no law against making a policeman angry and he cannot charge a man with offending him. Until the citizen acts overtly in violation of the law, he should take no action against him, least of all lower himself to the level of the citizen by berating and demeaning him in a loud and angry voice. The officer who withstands angry verbal assaults builds his own character and raises the standards of the department.

Those views expressed by Wilson are accepted by all responsible police officials. Although all departments have written regulations setting standards of behavior for their members, these regulations in many departments are too general. Where standards are violated, a thorough investigation should be made, and prompt, visible disciplinary action should be taken where justified.

[16]Ibid.
[17]O. W. Wilson, *Police Administration* (New York: McGraw-Hill Book Company, 1963), p. 9.

The Police and the Community

It is extremely difficult for police organizations to construct codes or rules dictating the specific manner in which all police tasks should be performed in order always to achieve public approval. The problems of police service are many, and they are subject to the influences of the constant development of public opinion in the community. Furthermore, police officers are continually deluged with new orders, directives, and advice, much of it conflicting and confusing. "Be firm but fair . . ." "Use caution . . ." "Assert yourself and be consistent . . ." "Address everyone as Mister, Miss, or Mrs. . . ." "You will be expected to attend community-relations classes."

In view of the importance of police work to every citizen in the community, it is necessary that police administrators develop and articulate clear policies aimed at guiding or governing the way policemen behave on the street. In the chapters that follow, we seek to analyze the relationships of the police and the community in perspective of history, to alert law enforcement personnel to the explosive potential in the mixture of urban violence and police power, and to detail possible solutions for the problem of confrontation between police power and community strife.

The Problem of Police Image in a Changing Community

Nature and Scope of the Problem

These are extremely difficult times for police, especially in the cities. Race riots have exposed them to personal peril and public controversy. And court decisions that have limited the use of confessions and have otherwise restricted police procedures, have greatly hampered the police in making cases against suspects.

In riots, the police duty is to try to keep order. In many disturbances, they have been under orders for long periods to endure snipers and fire bombers without retaliating. When the police do shoot back, some denounce them as murderers. When they use force to subdue rioters, some raise the cry of police brutality. In the dangerous confusion of riots, the conduct of some policemen has, no doubt, been excessive; some have definitely over-reacted. But it is clear that the police draw criticism from one side or another no matter what they do. Of course, the conduct of policemen in these dreadful moments is terribly important, and the dilemmas of precisely how they should behave are troubling indeed. It is very doubtful that there is any real concensus in this society about the right and wrong way to put down a riot, and, surely, this general uncertainty is reflected in many police departments. Some policemen have shot looters; others have chased and arrested them; still others have ignored them. In New York, police agreed to demands that several patrolmen be removed from rooftops above unruly crowds; in Cleveland, the Mayor withdrew most of the police from the troubled areas in the hope that community leaders could settle the problem; and in Newark, police (with national guardsmen and state troopers) were restricted from using any possible force at their disposal. In none of these instances did the approach chosen alleviate the problem. Needless to say, then, the balance of discretion in the midst of fierce action is delicate, and a police officer, as easily as any member of society, can tip that balance.

chapter

2

Fig. 2.1 There are situations, specifically when policemen and/or members of the fire-fighting department come under sniper fire, when it is necessary for police to use any possible force or fire power at their disposal. Photo courtesy of the San Francisco Police Department.

The events that touch off riots are not their real causes. The causes are rooted more deeply in the neighborhood, the community, the family, and the times in which we live. Once this type of disturbance begins, it snowballs at a fantastic rate, and soon thousands of citizens are in the streets, fires are started, windows are smashed, looting is widespread, and the police are faced with trying to control the frenzied mobs.

Riots and Civil Disobedience Are Not New Problems

Mob violence has been part of the history of the United States and other countries for many centuries. Civil disobedience has, therefore, existed as a law enforcement problem in one form or another down through the centuries, and has undoubtedly existed as a police problem in our country for as long a period as we have had police. Perhaps, civil disobedience is indigenous to a society which was largely founded

Nature and Scope of the Problem

by dissenters and was from the beginning dedicated to freedom of expression and of conscience.

J. E. Curry and G. D. King stated in their book, *Race Tension and the Police*, that violence has changed very little through the years. Many of the contemporary disturbances in the United States are similar in many respects to the disturbances and revolts in America throughout its history.

Thomas J. Fleming truly captures the picture in an article tracing the history of riots in the United States:[1] *Daniels Shays Rebellion* in Massachusetts (1786); *The Whiskey Wildness* (1792) in which 70,000 citizens of four western counties of Pennsylvania opposed the federal tax on whiskey enacted in 1791; *Nat Turner's Revolt* (1831) in the State of Virginia; *The Draft Riots* in New York City (1863); *The "Native Born" versus Immigration* riots which occurred in Philadelphia (1844); *The Great Railroad Strikes* of 1873 in which nonunionized workers "struck" the four largest railroads—the Baltimore and Ohio, the Pennsylvania, the New York Central, and the Erie—when, in two full days of rioting, more than 35 persons were killed, thousands were injured, and property damage totaled in the millions; *The "Industrial" Army* of unemployed led by Jacob Coxey, who with his followers of 1,200 protestors marched to Washington, D.C. Throughout the years Americans have often answered repression with violence; our riots today are not a new problem.

Riots, mob disturbances, and complete rebellion do not represent the entire historical scope of disturbances in the United States. The historical incidents, as presented above are only a small portion of disturbances which have occurred in the United States. Riots and civil strife have always been a major concern to the public and the fear of anarchy has always been prevalent in our society.

The Changing American Scene[2]

America, according to population experts and the National Advisory Commission on Civil Disorders, is divided

[1]T. J. Fleming, "Revolt in America," *This Week*, United Newspapers Magazine Corp., Sept. 1, 1968 ©, pp. 2–8.

[2]Much of the information in this section was adapted, with the permis-

into two societies—black and white, separate and unequal.

The problems of crime control, in general, and law enforcement, in particular, are always results of the change in social scenes. The dimensions and substance of community life are in such wholesale and radical transformation in our time, that we should pause and reflect on the influences that are modifying the conditions of our communities and posing new problems for the agencies of law enforcement. Cities are more and more becoming the residence of lower-class Negro groups while whites are moving to the suburbs. These settlement patterns have brought with them problems of housing and problems of income. Discontent and deprivation are an expression of these shifts in population distribution.

The view law enforcement has of minority groups is often a result of the attitude these groups take toward law enforcement. Attitudes on both sides must change. If law enforcement programs ignore the conditions which have motivated the behavior of minority groups, then police officers will continue many times to act in ways that invite hostility, anger, and, indeed, outright violence.

Racial Violence:
A Problem or a Product?

The general view of antisocial behavior as applied to mob violence holds that such actions are not in and of themselves the problem but, instead, a product of various social conditions (mob behavior will be covered extensively in a later chapter). This view eloquently justifies the fact that some individuals in all societies and in all classes of society respond to economic, social, and psychological pressure by violent acting-out behavior.

Although violence is something to be expected when social change is rapid, the President's Commission on Civil Disorders found that in 1967 "typical" violence or disorders did not take place. The disorders were unusual, irregular,

sion of N. A. Watson, I.A.C.P., from: D. J. Lohman, "Race Tension and Conflict" in N. A. Watson, ed., *Police and the Changing Community* (Wash., D.C.: International Association of Chiefs of Police, 1965), pp. 42–47.

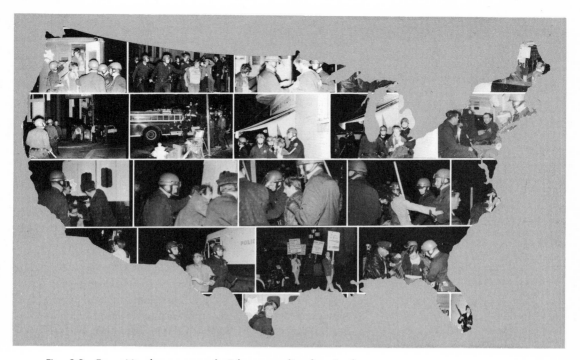

Fig. 2.2 Few cities have escaped violence or disorders in the United States. The tragic violence and bloodshed in the streets are only symptoms of deeper social problems and, to a considerable extent, the police are the victims of social problems which are not of their making. Photos courtesy of the San Francisco Police Department.

complex, and unpredictable social processes. Like most human events, they did not unfold in an orderly sequence. However, an analysis by the Commission leads to some conclusions about the riot process:

> The civil disorders of 1967 involved Negroes acting against local symbols of white American society, authority, and property in Negro neighborhoods—rather than against white persons.
>
> Of 164 disorders reported during the first nine months of 1967, eight (5 percent) were major in terms of violence and damage; 33 (20 percent) were serious but not major; 123 (75 percent) were minor and undoubtedly would not have received national attention as "riots" had the nation not been sensitized by the more serious outbreaks.

Racial Violence: A Problem or a Product?

In the 75 disorders studied by a Senate Subcommittee, 83 deaths were reported. Eighty-two percent of the deaths and more than half the injuries occurred in Newark and Detroit. About 10 percent of the dead and 38 percent of the injured were public employees, primarily the law officers and firemen. The overwhelming majority of the persons killed or injured in all the disorders were Negro civilians.

Initial damage estimates were greatly exaggerated. In Detroit, newspaper damage estimates at first ranged from $200,000,000 to $500,000,000; the highest recent estimate is $45,000,000. In Newark, early estimates ranged from $15,000,000 to $25,000,000. A month later, damage was estimated at $10,200,000, over 80 percent in inventory losses.[3]

The white population in the United States often comfort themselves with the thought that the black rage which pours out of the ghetto each summer in paroxysms of rioting and looting is the work of the "misfits" and "riffraff." However, a special study made for the Kerner Commission by Robert M. Fogelson, Professor of History at MIT, and Robert B. Hill, of the Bureau of Applied Social Research at Columbia University, disproves the "misfit-riffraff theory." In the Newark, Detroit, Dayton, Cincinnati, Grand Rapids, and New Haven riots, Commission study groups ascertained that three-fourths of the rioters had jobs and more than two-thirds were over 18 years of age. Many were women. While 44 to 90 percent of the men arrested did have criminal records, Hill and Fogelson point out that it is very easy to get a police record in a ghetto, and as for the "immigrant" theory, the Kerner Commission researchers found that the lifetime residents of the ghetto are the ones most likely to riot.

The tragic violence in American cities, the eruption of the ghettos, the bloodshed in the streets, the agonized cries for jobs and justice cannot be understood out of their historical context. They cannot be understood simply as a consequence of white racism or black rebellion. They cannot be controlled or eliminated by programs of slum clearance or social welfare or by crash programs to find jobs for the unemployed. The problems can be understood and managed only

[3]*Report of the National Advisory Commission on Civil Disorders* (Wash., D.C.: U.S. Government Printing Office, 1968), p. 3.

Nature and Scope of the Problem

if they are viewed as the consequence of profound disruption of traditional relationships between men and the land around them.

Technological changes in agriculture—primarily the replacement of man by machines—have uprooted masses of farm workers and driven them to the cities to seek the precarious refuge in the slums and ghettos. Thus far, American leaders appear to be unable to handle this problem.

State legislatures and the United States House of Representatives have refused to reapportion themselves sufficiently as the population has moved from farm to town, and have become "a barrier to progress." To most, the urban problem means the Negro problem; commissions, federal and local, have investigated it. But it does not take all that research to understand why it exists. It is common knowledge that the American Negro has been in this country for three and one-half centuries. He spent two and one-half centuries in slavery; he spent half a century in the rural slum South with unfulfilled promises of the Emancipation Proclamation. He spent another half century in the slums and ghettos of metropolitan United States, both North and South.

Furthermore, in recent decades, rising expectations have not been matched with anything real. Federal Civil Rights actions have not been followed through on the state and local level, and conditions have remained essentially the same.

The Profile of a Rioter

Studies show that those involved in riots were not preponderantly wild adolescents, hoodlums, racial extremists, and radical agitators, as is sometimes asserted, although such people undoubtedly took part. They were more or less a representative cross section of the Negro community, particularly of its young men, many of whom had lived in the neighborhood for many years and were steadily employed:

> The typical rioter in the year of 1967 was a Negro, unmarried male, between the ages of 15 and 24, in many ways very different from the stereotypes. He was not a migrant, he was born in the state and was a life-long resident of the

city in which the riot took place. Economically, his position was about the same as his Negro neighbor who did not actively participate in the riots.

Although he had not, usually, graduated from high school, he was somewhat better educated than the average innercity Negro, having at least attended high school for a time.

He feels strongly that he deserves a better job, that he is barred from achieving it, not because of lack of training, ability, or ambition, but because of discrimination by employers.

He rejects the white bigot's stereotype of the Negro as ignorant and shiftless. He takes great pride in his race and believes that in some respects Negroes are superior to the whites. He is extremely hostile to whites, but his hostility is more apt to be a product of social and economic clash than of race; he is almost equally hostile toward middle-class Negroes.

He is substantially better informed about politics than Negroes who were not involved in the riots. He is more likely to be actively engaged in civil right efforts, but he is extremely distrustful of the political system and of the political leaders.[4]

The Commission Report, furthermore, showed that many of those who participated in the riots, when questioned subsequently about their motives, stated quite explicitly that they had been protesting against, indeed trying to call the attention of the white community to, police misconduct, commercial exploitation and economic deprivation, and racial discrimination (see Chart One).

It is ironic that segregation in the United States today, after the passage of the antisegregation laws, is far more widespread than when segregation legally existed. One reason, of course, is that greater numbers of people are involved. The second and more important reason is that a subtle *de facto* system of discrimination has come into existence. The practice of subtle discrimination is persuasive, and it often serves as a more accurate measure of the attitudes of individuals than an expressed declaration to members of minority groups. A whole generation is now living under much more segregated conditions than their forebears. These conditions are prevalent throughout the country, and they refute the widespread

[4]*Report of the National Advisory Commission on Civil Disorders*, p. 73.

Nature and Scope of the Problem

Chart One (Part I)

Weighted Comparison of Grievance Categories*

	1st Place (4 Points)		2nd Place (3 Points)		3rd Place (2 Points)		4th Place (1 Point)		Total	
	Cities	Points	Cities	Points	Cities	Points	Cities	Points	Cities	Points
Police Practices	8	31½	4	12	0	0	2	2	14	45½
Unemployment & Under-Employment	3	11	7	21	4	7	3	3	17	42
Inadequate Housing	5	18½	2	6	5	9½	2	2	14	36
Inadequate Education	2	8	2	6	2	4	3	3	9	21
Poor Recreation Facilities	3	11	1	2½	4	7½	0	0	8	21
Political Structure and Grievance Mechanism	2	8	1	3	1	2	1	1	5	14
White Attitudes	0	0	1	3	1	1½	2	2	4	6½
Administration of Justice	0	0	0	0	2	3½	1	1	3	4½
Federal Programs	0	0	1	2½	0	0	0	0	1	2½
Municipal Services	0	0	0	0	1	2	0	0	1	2
Consumer and Credit Practices ..	0	0	0	0	0	0	2	2	2	2
Welfare	0	0	0	0	0	0	0	0	0	0

*The total of points for each category is the product of the number of cities times the number of points indicated at the top of each double column except where two grievances were judged equally serious. In these cases the total points for the two rankings involved were divided equally (e.g., in case two were judged equally suitable for the first priority, the total points for first and second were divided, and each received 3½ points).

RESULTS OF WEIGHTED COMPARISON OF GRIEVANCE CATEGORIES*

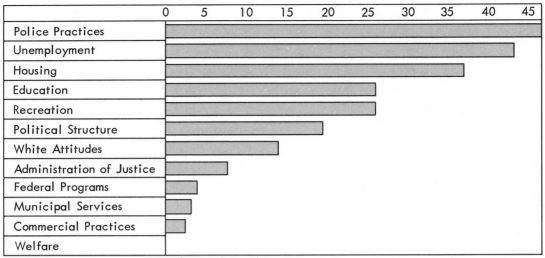

	0	5	10	15	20	25	30	35	40	45
Police Practices										
Unemployment										
Housing										
Education										
Recreation										
Political Structure										
White Attitudes										
Administration of Justice										
Federal Programs										
Municipal Services										
Commercial Practices										
Welfare										

* See right hand column of Chart 1 (Part 1).

SOURCE: *Report of the National Advisory Commission on Civil Disorders.*

idea that progress in residential desegration has been made in which Negroes should take satisfaction.

Riots: Implications for Impact on Law Enforcement

"Police work" is a phrase that conjures up in some minds a dramatic contest between a policeman and a criminal in which the party with the stronger arm or the craftier wit prevails. When a particularly desperate or dangerous criminal must be hunted down and brought to justice, there are heroic moments in the police work, but the situations that most policemen deal with most of the time are of quite another order. Much of American crime, delinquency, and disorder is associated with a complexity of social conditions: poverty, racial antagonism, family breakdown, or restlessness of young people. During the last 20 years, these conditions have been aggravated by such profound social changes as

Nature and Scope of the Problem

the technological and civil rights revolutions, and the rapid decay of innercities into densely packed, turbulent slums and ghettos.

It is in the cities that the conditions of life are the worst, that social tensions are the most acute, that riots occur, that crime rates are the highest, that the fear of crime and the demand for effective action against it are the strongest. This is not to say, however, that the crime rates have shown an increase only in the big cities of the United States. Actually, crime has shown a drastic increase everywhere in the United States. Serious crimes soared last year across the nation, according to a nationwide summary of the police statistics gathered by the Federal Bureau of Investigation.

One of the most fully documented facts about crime is that the common, serious crimes that worry people the most —murder, forcible rape, robbery, aggravated assault, and burglary—happen most often in the slums of large cities. Studies in city after city, in all regions of the country, have traced the variations in the rates for these crimes. The results, with monotonous regularity, showed that the offenses, the victims, and the offenders were found most frequently in the poorest, the most deteriorated, and the most socially disorganized areas of cities.

Studies of the crime rate in cities and of the conditions most commonly associated with high crime rates have been conducted for well over a century in Europe, and for many years in the United States. The findings have been remarkably consistent. Burglary, robbery, and serious assaults occur in areas characterized by low income, physical deterioration, dependency, racial and ethnic concentrations; broken homes, working mothers, low levels of education and vocational skills, high unemployment, high proportion of single males, overcrowded and sub-standard housing, high rates of tuberculosis and infant mortality, low rates of home ownership or single-family dwellings, and high population density. Studies that have mapped the relationship of these factors and crime have found them following the same pattern from one area of the city to another.

Crime rates in American cities tend to be highest in the city center and to decrease in relationship to distance from the center. This pattern has been found to hold fairly well for both offenses and offenders, although it is sometimes broken by unusual features of geography, enclaves of socially well-

Riots: Implications for Impact on Law Enforcement

integrated ethnic groups, irregularities in the distribution of opportunities to commit crime, and unusual concentrations of commercial and industrial establishments in outlying areas. The major irregularity found in the clustering of offenses and offenders beyond city boundaries is satellite areas that are developing such characteristics of the central city as high population mobility, commercial and industrial concentrations, low economic status, broken families, and other social problems.

The big city slum has always exacted its toll from its inhabitants, except where those inhabitants are bound together by an intensive social and cultural solidarity that provides a collective defense against the pressures of slum living. Several slum settlements inhabited by people of oriental ancestry have shown a unique capacity to do this. However, the common experience of the great numbers of immigrants of different racial and ethnic backgrounds who have poured into the poorest areas of our large cities has been quite different.

An historic series of studies by Clifford R. Shaw and Henry D. McKay, of the Institute of Juvenile Research in Chicago, documents the disorganizing impact of slum life on different groups of immigrants as they moved through the slums and struggled to gain an economic and social foothold in the city. Throughout the period of immigration, areas with high delinquency and crime rates kept this high rate, even though members of new nationality groups moved in to displace the older residents. Each nationality group showed high rates of delinquency among its members who were living near the center of the city and lower rates for those living in the better, outlying residential areas. Also, for each nationality group, those living in the poor areas had more of all the other social problems commonly associated with life in the slums.

This same pattern of high crime rates in the slum neighborhoods and low crime rates in the better districts is true among the Negroes and members of other minority groups who have made up the most recent waves of migration to the big cities (see Table 1). (Minority groups and crime will be discussed in another chapter.) As other groups before them, they have had to crowd into areas where they can afford to live while they search for ways to live better. The disorganizing personal and social experiences of life in the slums are producing the same problems for the new minority group

Nature and Scope of the Problem

Two and one-half times more whites than Negroes were arrested in 1967 for all crimes. During the same year, 5402 whites were arrested for criminal homicide compared to 5512 Negroes for the same crime.

Last year 34,713 Negroes were arrested for possession of weapons compared to 31,977 whites.

In 1967, approximately 30 percent of all arrests of whites and Negroes were for drunkenness. However, 70 percent of the arrests of Indians were for drunkenness. Incidentally, the Indians referred to in the report are American Indians.

Arrests By Race for 1967

RACE	Under 18 Years	Over 18 Years	Total By Race
White	929,204	2,701,583	3,630,787
Negro	322,127	1,140,429	1,462,556
Indian	10,086	111,312	121,398
Chinese	434	1,292	1,726
Japanese	1,177	2,313	3,490
All Others	13,586	31,759	45,345
TOTAL	1,276,614	3,988,583	5,265,302

Breakdown of arrests by race (source: FBI).

residents, including high rates of crime and delinquency. As they acquire a stake in urban society and move into better areas in the city, the crime rates and the incidents of other social problems drop to lower levels.

Riots: Implications for Impact on Law Enforcement

Social
Problems
and
Constitutional
Government: Impact on Law Enforcement

Chapter Two discussed the nature and scope of certain social problems that affect law enforcement. The very nature of these problems suggests further discussion of a number of significant influences, not the least of which are wars, student revolt, crime, and the *rate* of social change. Examination of these significant influences on social change, however, may gain greater clarity through a study of the specific restrictions imposed on law enforcement by government in general, and by Constitutional government in particular. It will be seen throughout this volume that the complexity of enforcing law has increased steadily with the advent of the Magna Charta, Bill of Rights, and Fourth Amendment, all of which have molded the foundation of modern Constitutional government.

But complex or not, law enforcement has one function that has remained consistent in all governments throughout history: the promotion of an orderly environment. In meeting this governmental function, Constitutional government more than any other governmental form, must take into consideration the relationship between societal power and the power of man's will. Most of what is called "the wisdom of the ages" probably deals with this very relationship in one way or another. So also does this very relationship define most of our "social problems." For in the final analysis, the individual power of the person is equally potent whether in support of, or in dissent from, the provision of an orderly environment—"orderly environment" being increasingly defined in terms that transcend the mere provision of personal safety and property security.

chapter

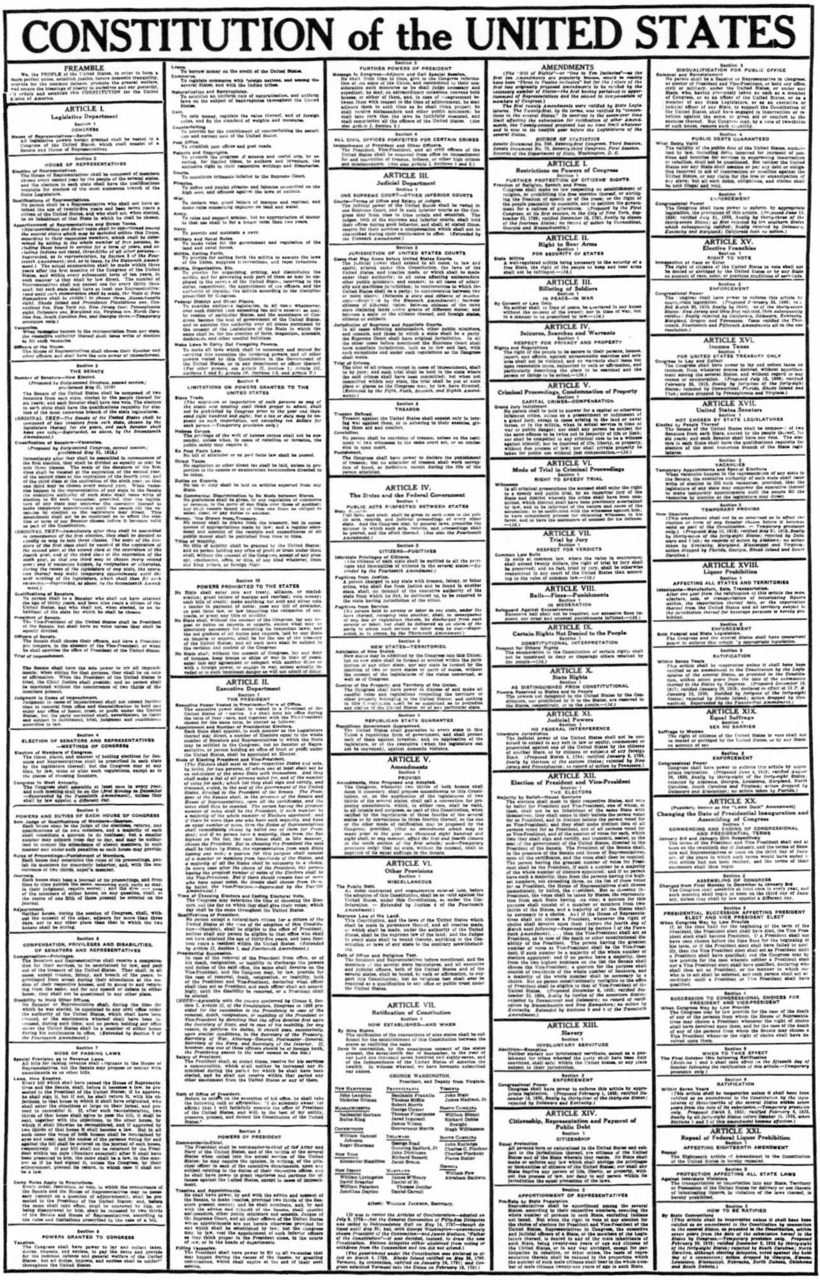

CONSTITUTION of the UNITED STATES

Published by GEORGE BURR MacANNAN, Taft Building, Hollywood, California. For Best Results this Parchment Should Be Mounted on White Backing.

Fig. 3.1

For or Against
Existing Government

The subject of war is frequently discussed as one of many major influences on social conditions defined as problems, particularly when these influences are defined as problems involving societal power and the power of an individual's *will*. Examples such as the social implications of the Korean and Vietnamese conflicts are appropriate to such discussions, as of course is the gross impact of World War II on American society.

But in terms of whether the individual is "for" existing (established) government or against it, problems such as these would appear likely to influence "against" government, if for no other reason than the jeopardy in which the government's existing system of providing orderly environment is placed by changes during war. Social congestion, decline in family functioning, increases in delinquency and mental illness are but a few of the many changes that usually accompany war.[1]

In attempting to solve social problems such as those that accompany war, existing governments ("the establishment") often find themselves choosing between two rather restrictive alternatives: *suppressing change* or *making change*. The degree of opposition—from those seeking solution of social problems through change—will be directly related to the degree of suppression.

Governmental reaction to social problems, whether induced by wartime or other factors, is of crucial interest to law enforcement. Governmental suppression of change has conspicuous implications in this context, but so also has governmental decision to make changes. Determination of precisely *what* changes are being sought, and by whom they are being sought, frequently becomes a concern to law enforcement, whether law enforcement desires this involvement or not. Student revolt, while only one of myriad signs of unrest, might serve as an example of how law enforcement becomes involved in social problems and governmental efforts to retain an orderly environment.

[1] J. Nordskog, E. McDonagh, M. J. Vincent (eds.), *Analyzing Social Problems*, (New York: Dryden Press, 1950), p. 689.

Social Problems and Constitutional Government

Student Unrest

The notion of student nonconformity is by no means new, and for this reason it may be somewhat questionable as an example of unrest, government control, and law enforcement involvement. Indeed, even before pantie raids and goldfish swallowing, most college campuses had accumulated a history of incidents in which segments of the student body had drawn attention to themselves through nonconformity. But insofar as "the establishment" was concerned, there remained little reason to believe that questions were being raised about the very system that was responsible for providing an orderly environment.

A somewhat different pattern of dissent began to emerge on college campuses approximately the same time of enrollment by children whose parents had been directly involved in World War II. The changing pattern of dissent had, by the early 1960s, drawn mass attention through student demonstrations in support of demands ranging from "free-speech" to preventing campus recruitment by military or defense industries. The deluge of publicity on draft-card burning dramatized the increasing blame placed on "the establishment" as the source of considerable student unrest and serves as the rationale for considering student nonconformity as relevant to government interest in the subject of unrest.

In the spring of 1968, a survey by the National Student Association noted 221 demonstrations on 101 campuses across the nation, 59 cases involving the virtual take-over of an administration building. At the October, 1968, convention held at the University of Colorado by the Students for a Democratic Society (SDS), a call was made for a national student strike to support demonstrations geared to disrupt the pending presidential election. The widely publicized problems erupting at the major political conventions were seen as profound comments on the magnitude of unrest. So also have been the violent outbreaks on campuses since—Columbia University and San Francisco State College serving as particularly salient examples beginning in 1968.

Of course, student revolt is merely one sign of unrest, and only one social problem. Many other social problems, perhaps of greater immediate concern to law enforcement, are dealt with elsewhere in this book. But student revolt, as it

For or Against Existing Government

functions in a Constitutional government that guarantees the right of dissent, may provide many clues to the process of interpreting social tension, a process of vital importance to the police in an ever-changing society.

Interpreting Social Tension:
A Matter of Degree

If there were a time when pantie raids by college students were thought to be the behavior of "extremists," then the nature of current student nonconformity modifies this view. The relatively innocuous degree to which pantie raids might be identified as extreme can be seen readily by examining the relative militancy in the student activities relating to "the establishment" and still more clearly seen by examining the philosophical position of the Third World, Black Panthers, or the earlier Black Muslims. The degrees of extremity in racially oriented student unrest can be further clarified by comparing the philosophical position of the Black Panthers with that of the National Association for the Advancement of Colored People (NAACP) or perhaps with the views espoused by the late Reverend Dr. Martin Luther King. Depending on the views and orientation of the observer, the views of any or all of the foregoing could be called "extreme" —whether on campus or off. The *degree* of demand for change might, therefore, prove a more effective way of assessing the potential impact on law enforcement.

Our quick and violent social changes might well make today's extremist or activist tomorrow's conservative. This becomes important, because interpreting social tension requires a distinction between consequential and inconsequential patterns for change.

Student unrest in itself may or may not be of consequence to law enforcement inasmuch as student unrest frequently relates to matters totally beyond the scope of law enforcement. As an example, how a student feels about his grades is of little concern to police. Yet students, whether happy or unhappy with grades, become of concern to police when gathering in large groups violently demonstrating to deny local draft boards access to grade records.

Anticipating the severity and degree of student unrest

Social Problems and Constitutional Government

requires some understanding of such matters as the virtual certainty that bureaucracy, colleges included, treats individuals as abstractions or statistics rather than as persons. This being the case, a student's concern about grades may often be merely a symptom of the problem rather than the problem itself. But the student concerned enough about grades or other scholastic problems usually raises another meaningful issue —the issue of relevance.[2] Grades then, though not of immediate police concern, might conceivably become the initial stages of developing a degree of unrest that is of concern to law enforcement. As an aside, the inhabitants of ghettos customarily express dissatisfaction with public-assistance and other "establishment" programs prior to violent outbursts, such as the large-scale riots occurring in many metropolitan areas throughout the United States in the past decade. Recognizing complaints about public assistance in the ghetto, or concerning oneself with unrest with grades escalating into the subject of *relevance*, may be one method by which law enforcement may anticipate as well as interpret the degree of social tension. For whether it be the ghetto inhabitant's desire for sufficient political and economic power to modify a system that seems to continue relegation, or a student's desire for a college education that is "relevant" to his needs in a changing society, the degree of dissatisfaction with the "established" system for answering these problems is necessarily the most accurate measure of impending need for police concern. So while college grades would seem outside the scope of the police, students' collective decision that they will not be "graded" for subjects that fail to meet the needs of either the student or the society may well evolve into a clearly defined law-enforcement matter. The additional inertia provided by the fact that these same grades might influence a selective military system provides still further reason to believe that police intervention may ultimately be required.

For law enforcement the question becomes one of over-all governmental response to mounting demands—a frequently difficult problem in Constitutional forms of government. Police interest in the development stage of social unrest, whether on the campus or in the ghetto or anywhere in the community, can no longer be denied. In an era of increasing demands, the jeopardy of violence continues to

[2]Western Interstate Commission for Higher Education, *WICHE*, Vol. XV, No. 1, Nov., 1968, pp. 3–7.

For or Against Existing Government

mount, and the strain on police to provide an orderly environment becomes a more consistent variable in the field of law enforcement.

Other Factors in Orderly Environment in Constitutional Government

It has been persuasively argued that "amid disturbing social, political, and economic conditions," our society is virtually "on trial."[3] In effect this argument pictures society as approaching either success or failure in evolving relevant legal processes within the Constitutional frame of government.

Legal process, including both legislative and judicial, is isolated as the crucially significant variable because it is this process that determines governmental response to the mounting social tensions and demands previously discussed.

The judicial process, particularly Supreme Court decisions, necessarily flows almost entirely from the legislative process. But the power of the legislative process notwithstanding, it remains abundantly clear that the judicial process through Supreme Court decisions has had far more *direct* effect and dramatic impact on law enforcement than any other single aspect of governmental response to social change. For this reason, the Supreme Court decisions and related decisions become a major factor in assessing law enforcement rule in a changing society.

Supreme Court Decisions

It has been said that American courts function as social controls of values and attitudes toward law while at the same time reconciling grievances—grievances between either the state and the individual, or between individuals.[4] And while the press has carried prominent articles about the need for strong judicial measures on behalf of the state in every decade

[3]W. Freeman, *Society on Trial* (Springfield, Ill.: Charles C Thomas, Publisher, 1965), Preface.

[4]W. Amos, and C. Wellford, *Delinquency Prevention* (Englewood Cliffs, N.J.: Prentice-Hall, Inc., 1967), p. 208.

Social Problems and Constitutional Government

for the past 50 years,[5] it is only in recent times that general concern has focused directly on the other responsibility to reconcile grievances between individuals and the state.

A traditional role of law enforcement in Constitutional forms of government is *apprehending* law violators, leaving *punishment* to the judicial process. Philosophically, at least, such a role permits the *prevention* of crime to be a mutual, although secondary, responsibility of both police and courts. But in recent times, both police and courts are increasingly faced with "crimes" stemming from growing demands for social reform, rather than with those merely violating criminal statute. One apparent reaction by the court, particularly the Supreme Court, has been a number of decisions tending to have great impact on police procedure in general, and with the relationship of police to social change in particular. In effect, the Supreme Court has handed down rulings that not only judge the lower courts' functions but further judge the police function as well.

Much of the basis for the increasing Supreme Court assessment of police practice is the Fourth Constitutional Amendment, and to some degree the Ninth Amendment. The implications of the Fourth Amendment for the police function have received more than adequate concern in the literature.[6] Nonetheless, a brief review of the historical court highlights referred to in Chapter Four may serve to clarify this issue.

In 1914 the United States Supreme Court ruled in the *Weeks vs. U.S.* case that a federal court could not accept evidence that was obtained in violation of "search and seizure" protection, guaranteed by the Fourth Amendment. In 1963 the Supreme Court ruled on the appeal case of *Gideon vs. Wainwright*. The effect of this ruling was that new trials could be demanded by anyone convicted of crime without legal counsel. Moving closer to the functions of police, a 1964 decision was handed down in the case of *Escobedo vs. Illinois*. This decision, based on a five to four majority, interpreted the Constitutional rights of an indigent to include legal

---

[5]R. W. Winslow, *Crime in a Free Society* (Encino, Calif.: Dickenson Pub. Co., Inc., 1968).

[6]E. L. Barrett, "Personal Rights, Property Rights, and the Fourth Amendment, " *1960 Supreme Court Review* (Chicago: University of Chicago Press, 1961), p. 65. See also, C. R. Sowle, ed., *Police Power and Individual Freedom* (Springfield, Ill.: Charles C Thomas, Publisher, 1962); and W. H. Parker, "Birds Without Wings," *The Police Yearbook*, 1965 (Wash., D.C.: International Chiefs of Police).

Other Factors in Orderly Environment in Constitutional Government

counsel at the time of police interrogation. In 1966 the court ruled in the *Miranda vs. Arizona* that persons "suspected" of crimes were entitled to legal counsel during interrogation. These interpretations of Constitutional rights placed law enforcement in the position of viewing many traditional investigative methods as "unconstitutional." If Constitutional rights are violated by certain heretofore practiced police methods, the question becomes one of alternate approaches.

Alternate approaches are at best difficult when the overall function of the court itself is undergoing change—whether or not the change flows from precisely the same Supreme Court decisions directly affecting police. The magnitude of change in the court process is examined clearly in a report by the President's Commission on Law Enforcement and the Administration of Justice:

> Some Constitutional limitations on the criminal court are based on principals common to most civilized criminal systems. One is that criminal penalties may be imposed only in response to a specific act that violates a pre-existing law. The criminal court cannot act against persons out of apprehension that they may commit crimes, but only against persons who have already done so. Furthermore, the basic procedures of the criminal court must conform to concepts of "due process" that have grown from English, common law seeds. Unquestionably, adherence to due process complicates, and in many instances handicaps, the work of the courts. But the law rightly values due process over efficient process. And by permitting the accused to challenge its fairness and legality at every stage of his prosecution, the system provides the occasion for the law to develop in accordance with changes in society and society's ideals. . . . Nevertheless, these limitations on prosecution are the product of two centuries of Constitutional development in this country. They are integral parts of a system for balancing the interests of the individual and the state that has served the nation well.[7]

If at least the goal of the judicial process is "a system for balancing the interests of the individual and the state," then the definition of what these interests actually are becomes important. The particular importance of such definition to law enforcement is clearly implied in the evolution of Supreme Court decisions geared not to remedy judicial pro-

[7]*The Challenge of Crime in a Free Society*, p. 125.

Social Problems and Constitutional Government

cedure, but rather to relieve social problems—relief that frequently requires police to abandon traditional police methods.

But regardless of the importance of defining these specific interests, definitions are not easy in an era of articulate yet divergent explanations of interests. The difficulty of such definition is increased still more by Supreme Court decisions that influence not only the definition of what "due process" is, but also influence the definition of the interest served through "due process." Nevertheless, defining interests remains crucial to law enforcement.

Civil Rights and Power

Supreme Court decisions since World War II have influenced a number of interest-definitions—particularly, in terms of educational opportunity and civil rights. In the majority of Supreme Court treatments of opportunity and rights, there is an implied definition of the individual's interest in political power. For indeed, insofar as Constitutional government is concerned, there is little value in guaranteeing equal distribution of educational opportunity and civil rights if there is not a corresponding equality in the power to influence both. Put another way, the individual cannot gain equality in either educational opportunity or in civil rights unless and until he also commands as much political power as is necessary to guarantee both—at least in Constitutional forms of government. The absence of sufficient power to assure such influence has been persuasively isolated as the "center problem of the ghetto."[8]

Social problems of any kind are remedied or relieved through power—ideally through political or economic power or, in unfortunate extremes, through the power of violence. The absence of political and economic power most assuredly leads to resentment among those on whom social problems have the greatest direct impact. This resentment, whether expressed or implied, is of critical interest to law enforcement in an era marked by Supreme Court decisions and civil rights legislation tending in some instances merely to dramatize the frustration in achieving the power to influence one's own destiny.

[8]J. Barndt, *Why Black Power* (New York: Friendship Press, 1968), p. 31.

Other Factors in Orderly Environment in Constitutional Government

Equal Justice for Minority Groups

The court and the police are generally the first institutions of society that are examined when the idea of justice or injustice is mentioned. It appears that a more logical place to begin the examination would be by investigating minority group treatment within the general society. Because, by 1967, 70 percent of the people living within ghettos were members of minority groups,[1] the ghettos themselves need to be examined. A person of the slum ghetto is unable to enjoy the liberty or freedom to pursue many of his goals. Some study of ghetto life with the limitations it imposes upon its residents needs to be evaluated if we are to arrive at a better understanding of the subtleties of justice.

For the purpose of trying to understand the concept of ghettos, the example of the black ghetto will be used. The black ghetto is used here with the full knowledge that there are many ghettos with other ethnic compositions.

Almost every large city in the United States has a Negro ghetto. The ghettos are a constantly growing concentration of Negroes within the central city. There are several reasons for this ghetto-type segregation. Some of these are that Negroes, like other migrants and immigrants, first moved into the oldest sections of the city. Unlike the immigrants from Europe, the black man's color barred him from leaving those poor neighborhoods when he became financially able to do so. The predominantly white society which had absorbed the immigrant has, for the most part, refused to absorb the black man. This was done through local housing ordinances or real estate codes. It was even done by violence or intimidation. Often, when a black man moved into a white neighborhood, whites refused to remain and moved from that area, thereby

---

[1] *Report of the National Advisory Commission on Civil Disorders* (Wash., D.C.: U.S. Government Printing Office, 1968), p. 115.

chapter

4

causing vacancies which were, in turn, filled by black citizens, and the whole character of the neighborhood was changed. As the Negro ghetto within the city increased in size, white residents moved to the suburbs. This tended to increase residential segregation within the population.

Considering this unequal population distribution, an examination of the living conditions of minorities might well be in order at this point.

Housing and Economic Problems in the Ghetto

A federal government report indicates that despite the fact that federal housing has been in existence since 1934, housing is still one of the greatest problems of the urban poor.[2] The same report indicates that two-thirds of the black Americans living in cities live in neighborhoods characterized by blight and sub-standard housing. Approximately 25 percent of the black population that lives in central cities lives in sub-standard housing, compared to 8 percent of all Caucasians. Black housing is far more likely to be overcrowded than is white housing, but Negroes tend to pay the same amount of money for this housing as Caucasians do for houses in better condition. Landlords often victimize the ghetto residents by ignoring building codes, probably because they know ghetto residents, by and large, are restricted due to economics or ethnic background to living in the ghetto.

Because of the low income earned by black people who live in ghettos, a large percentage of the family income is spent for housing. Needless to say, ghetto residents who must pay a larger percentage of their income for housing have much less money left over for other items. There is some feeling that ghetto residents might be able to leave the ghetto if they were able to earn a better income. However, low income, unemployment, and under-employment are among the most serious and persistent problems of the disadvantaged minorities and contribute to civil disorder in the ghettos.

Even more important than unemployment is the problem of the undesirable nature of many jobs open to Negroes. Often, Negro workers are concentrated in the lowest paying

[2]*Report of the National Advisory Commission on Civil Disorders*, p. 257.

Housing and Economic Problems in the Ghetto

Fig. 4.1 Ghetto housing, although substandard and over crowded, is exceedingly expensive in comparison with housing that is generally afforded to white persons.

and lowest skilled jobs in the economy. These jobs often involve sub-standard wages and uncertainty of steady employment. Residents of disadvantaged Negro neighborhoods, because of this, have been subject for decades to social, economic, and psychological disadvantages. The result tends to be a cycle of failure. The employment disabilities of one generation breed the same kind of problems in the following generation. This problem of unemployment and under-employment is further aggravated by the continual flow of new, unskilled, jobless migrants to the ghetto from rural areas.

These problems seem to be related to high crime rates, insecurity, and poor health and sanitation in the ghetto, areas that we will examine next.

Social and Health Problems in the Ghetto

For years, criminologists have known that crime rates are always higher in poor neighborhoods, whatever their ethnic composition. This is no exception in the Negro ghetto. The black residents' sense of personal security certainly is undermined by the frequent number of crimes found in the big city ghetto. Negroes in poor areas are probably more likely to be victims of major crimes than residents of most higher income areas.

Equal Justice for Minority Groups

The crimes in the ghetto are committed by a small minority of the residents. This means that most of the victims are law-abiding black people. In part, because of this high crime rate, many Negroes feel bitterly toward the police, feeling they do not receive adequate protection from law enforcement agencies.

Ghetto residents also have other problems. These poor families are usually found to have poor diets, poor housing, poor clothing, and poor medical care. Many of these families suffer from chronic health problems that will have adverse effects upon employment possibilities. Although Negro ghetto residents have many more health problems, they spend less than half as much per person on medical services as white families with comparable incomes.

Education in the Ghetto

A good education traditionally has been the means by which people have escaped from ignorance, poverty, and discrimination, and consequently from the ghetto. Therefore, education within the ghetto is a particularly acute problem. However, ghetto schools, for the most part, have failed to liberate the blacks from their plight. This failure has caused resentment and consequently, grievances by the black community against the ghetto schools.

The record of public education for ghetto children becomes worse as time passes. According to a government report, Negro children score 3.3 grades behind white students on standard achievement tests at the twelfth grade level.[3] Further, far more Negro students (and minority students in general) drop out of school than white students. Unfortunately, a very high proportion of the students who do not graduate are not equipped to enter the normal job market, and when they do, they tend to get low-skilled, low-paying jobs.

Generally speaking, ghetto schools are inferior in many respects to schools in predominantly white neighborhoods. The teachers tend to be less qualified and have less experience

[3]*Equality of Educational Opportunity*, U.S. Department of Health, Education and Welfare (Wash., D.C.: U.S. Government Printing Office, 1966), p. 20.

than teachers in suburban schools. Ghetto schools typically have overcrowded classrooms; the buildings are old and poorly equipped; the books and supplies are inadequate. Ghetto teachers indicate that they have more maladjusted students and fewer facilities to deal with these students. Another valid criticism of ghetto schools is that the curricula and material are usually geared to middle-class white suburban students, and the material tends to make no reference to Negro achievements or contributions to American life. *Because the school work has little or no relevance to the ghetto youngster's life experience, he concludes that education in general is not relevant to his life.*

Many of the black residents of the ghetto are angry about the inadequacies of their schools. Unfortunately, the communication between the community and the school administrators is quite poor. This can be attributed to the fact that teachers and administrators live outside the ghetto and do not fully understand the problems of the ghetto. The parents, lacking in formal education, feel they have little voice in changing school matters.

The school, employment, crime and health problems, as well as housing, all reflect the nature of the ghettos. These factors together are what make up the world of the ghetto.

The Typical Ghetto Family

The poorest people in the United States are found in the ghetto. A government report indicates that in 1966 approximately 12 percent of the country's white families were poor, while approximately 41 percent of the black families in the United States were poor.[4] Of the Negro poor, about 45 percent lived in ghettos.

Poverty has many effects on the ghetto family. Many of the men of the families cannot get in key jobs and are unable to support their families, and their status and self-respect are affected. Husbands tend to feel inadequate because their wives are forced to work. Often the wives are able to make more money than their husbands, and this in turn tends to make husbands feel even more inadequate;

[4]*Report of the National Advisory Commission on Civil Disorders, p. 127.*

consequently, they often separate from or divorce their wives.

Almost three times as many black families are fatherless as white families; therefore, there are many more black families than white families headed by females. Negro families headed by women are twice as likely to live in poverty as those headed by men. The lack of a father figure in a family has a negative impact upon the children. In ghettos, this problem of fatherless families has many side effects. For example, many children from poor families with their fathers gone and their mothers working to support the family spend much of their lives in the streets. In these streets, crime and violence are commonplace.

The real injustice of the ghetto system is that for many of the children, the future is almost hopeless. The great majority of these children are growing up under conditions that make them better candidates for crime and civil disorder than for jobs that would provide them an entry into the mainstream of the American economy.

Equal Justice Under the Law

An examination of the history of the treatment of minority groups under the law should give one some insight into the changes that have been made within slightly over one hundred years.

Table Two

Historical Highlights Related to Members of Minority Groups

The Dred Scott Decision (1857)	This decision indicated that a slave was not a citizen and that, consequently, he had no rights whatsoever in court.
The Fourteenth Amendment to the Constitution of the United States (1868)	This Amendment to the Constitution clearly states that members of a minority group are to be treated equally under the law.
Plessy v. Ferguson (1896)	The Supreme Court upheld the doctrine of separate but equal

Equal Justice under the Law

	rights as it related to the civil rights of American Negroes.
Brown *v.* The Board of Education (1954)	This decision by the Supreme Court indicated that the Court felt separate but equal facilities in education were illegal.
Gideon *v.* Wainwright (1963)	The Supreme Court established the precedent that a person charged with a felony shall have counsel even if he is too poor to pay for it. (Essentially, this meant that the State must pay for defense counsel for accused felons.)
Miranda *v.* Arizona (1966)	This decision made it mandatory that a person be forewarned about his rights under the Constitution. (The importance of this decision is that now poor minority group members were being told of their rights, the same rights that affluent and better educated people had been aware of all along.)
Gault *v.* Arizona (1967)	This court decision gave minors many of the rights that adults enjoy in the court process. (The importance of this is that from 40 to 50 percent of the persons arrested for crimes in the United States are juveniles, and an inordinate proportion of the persons arrested are from minority groups.)

Table Two indicates a change in the courts' philosophy regarding minorities in the last hundred years. All indications are that the courts have become more sympathetic to the problems of minorities. However, there are still some inadequacies that are in the process of being changed.

Criminal cases begin the process with an arrest, which is followed by detention until a magistrate can decide on what amount of bail the accused may post so that he can be released before trial. The economic fact of bail is such that

Equal Justice for Minority Groups

it discriminates and punishes the poor. The poor go to jail, while the affluent buy their freedom. Because of this, the poor often lose their jobs and their earning capacities. This all transpires before the trial and before there has been a determination of guilt or innocence. The end result is that a person, whether guilty or not, may be punished rather severely for being poor.

Alternatives to routine arrests and detention have been developed by several states and the federal courts. These alternatives generally have taken two forms. In the first situation, a judicial officer issues a *summons* on complaint of the prosecutor. In the second situation, a police officer issues a *citation* or notice to appear, much like a traffic citation. In both instances, the person is allowed to remain free in the community on his "own recognizance." This move by the courts has tended to offer a defendant the chance for fair treatment before trial, whether he is poor or rich.

According to Thomas E. Willinge, Professor of Law at the University of Toledo, the major barrier between poor people and justice in civil matters is expert legal counsel.[5] The poor person who comes to court feels he is being treated unjustly, and, therefore, he comes to court with what he thinks is a good cause. Generally speaking, lawyers represent the businessman against the poor person who has no lawyer. These lawyers generally win judgments against the poor. As a result, the poor tend to leave the courtroom as losers, without any feeling that justice has been done.

In most instances, the decision to initiate criminal prosecution is a matter of police judgment. Supposedly, this judgment is based upon the legal definition of crime. Often, it is quite clear that a violation of the law may occur and that the police may know of that violation, but they do not act. Some of the factors which cause this discrepancy are: *(1) The volume of criminal law violations and the limited resources of the police, (2) the enactment of laws which define criminal conduct in a most generalized manner, and (3) various pressures reflecting the attitudes of a particular community.*

An example of this dilemma is *social gambling*. In most jurisdictions, gambling is illegal. For the average white middle-class American, a small game of "poker" within the

---

[5]T. E. Willinge, "Financial Barriers and the Access of Indigents to the Courts," *The Georgetown Law Journal*, Vol. 57, No. 2, November, 1968, pp. 253–306.

Equal Justice under the Law

confines of one's own home is usually possible because the indoor living space is adequate. On the other hand, in the crowded ghetto where living space is at a premium because the average number of persons per room is so high, games of chance are often moved to streets or alleyways.

When police are informed of such games in the ghetto area, they generally respond and arrest the players. Police justify this intervention by saying these arrests serve as crime prevention functions because they know from past experience that these games frequently end in fights, while games of chance played in suburban areas generally do not.[6] Although the intentions of the police would appear to be responsible police work, this practice gives the appearance of class and racial discrimination.

A second example is the police handling of *assaultive-type offenses*. These offenses come to the attention of law enforcement agencies frequently because they occur in public or because the victim is found to be in need of medical aid. The perpetrator of the assault is known to the victim in a large percentage of the cases, yet there is frequently no arrest. If an arrest is made, it is often followed quickly by a release without prosecution. This practice of no prosecution is especially true in ghetto areas due, according to law enforcement personnel, primarily to the unwillingness on the part of victims to cooperate with the prosecution. Even if a victim cooperates at the investigation stage, his willingness to cooperate often disappears at the time of the trial. More success might be achieved at the trial phase if the victim were subpoenaed to testify. However, the subpoena process is seldom used. Instead, the path of least resistance is followed, and when the victim fails to appear to testify, prosecution is terminated. This action is rationalized on the grounds that the victim was the only party harmed and he does not wish to pursue the matter. Cases of this sort can be written off statistically as cleared cases which, in turn, are an index of police efficiency, but they do not accurately reflect police effectiveness.

When a ghetto resident attacks someone who is not a ghetto resident, vigorous prosecution is generally the result. Undoubtedly, this leads to the feeling by many ghetto resi-

[6]*Task Force Report: The Police*, A publication of the President's Commission on Law Enforcement and Administration of Justice (Wash., D.C.: U.S. Government Printing Office, 1967), pp. 21–22.

Fig. 4.2 Most assault within the ghetto occurs between residents of the particular area. Arrests and subsequent prosecution are rare. According to law enforcement personnel, their inability to arrest and prosecute is attributed to lack of cooperation on the part of victims, witnesses, and so on. Photo courtesy of the San Francisco Police Department.

dents that police tend to tolerate assaultive conduct in the ghetto but do not do so in other areas of the city. Furthermore, because of these kinds of incidents, Negroes firmly believe that police brutality and harassment occur repeatedly in ghetto neighborhoods.[7] This belief that the police tend to be unduly brutal when they arrest minority group members is probably one of the main reasons for minority group resentment against the police. Research shows that these complaints of police brutality are generally unjustified.[8]

[7]*Report of the National Advisory Commission on Civil Disorders*, p. 159.
[8]A. J. Reiss, Jr., "Police Brutality—Answers to Key Questions," *Trans-Action*, Vol. 5, No. 8, July/August, 1968, pp. 10–19.

Equal Justice under the Law

Physical abuse does not seem to be practiced against minority group members in a greater degree than it is practiced against majority group members. However, physical abuse is certainly not the only source of irritation to the ghetto resident. Any practice that degrades a citizen's status, restricts his freedom, or annoys or harasses him is felt to be an unjust use of police power.

Policemen who "talk down" to a person or call him names are objectionable to most citizens. Black citizens complain that law enforcement personnel also "talk down" to them by calling them "boy" or "man." Other objectionable practices include the use of profanity and abusive language toward minority group members. There is no doubt that such treatment strips people of their dignity.

All parties agree that the elimination of police misconduct requires care in the selection of police for ghetto areas. The police responsibility in these areas is particularly demanding and sensitive as well as frequently dangerous. The highest caliber of personnel is required if police in the ghetto are to overcome accusations of inadequate protection and discriminatory actions.

Social Change and Community Tension

Early American culture developed rurally for the most part. Without machinery, farmers in the north depended on the labor of their children; in the agrarian economy of the south, labor was provided by slaves. As prehistoric ancestors utilized the newly invented wheel and other tools, early rural Americans enjoyed many labor-saving devices, but the primary source of energy in this infant culture was man.

The transition from agriculture to industry, known as the Industrial Revolution, tended to displace both the northern children and the newly freed southern slaves toward cities—cities busily replacing human labor with machinery at an even faster pace than the mechanization that was occurring on rural farms.

One immediate result of the Industrial Revolution was increased leisure time for many. In the case of those who worked, the mechanization of labor reduced the amount of time needed to achieve desired production levels. For those unable to gain employment in urban factories, leisure time also increased dramatically, if not desirably—at least the "leisure" that was available during periods when employment was being sought. In either event, the dawn-til-dusk workday began to fade from the urban scene. With it also faded the security of the dreary but certain continuation of living out a predictable life on the farm or plantation. Several major wars and a never-ending elimination of jobs by machinery have done little to ensure the security of the modern urban worker—in spite of, and perhaps because of, ever-increasing leisure time.

Clearly, America has changed in other ways, but these changes that produce a greater abundance of leisure time clarify the sources of many social tensions.

chapter

5

Social Change

Change is often not optional. The Grand Canyon is becoming deeper at the rate of one inch per year, whether such change is approved of or not. Scotland moves toward Ireland about eight feet annually, while Europe and the United States are moving apart at about one foot per year. London sinks a fraction of an inch annually, while the North Pole moves southward by six inches.

When there are changes in the very tangible, physical world, then changes in the social world should be no surprise. Any difference in human behavior over a period of time is change—and difference in human behavior is constantly observable.

Leisure

Many, if not most, would agree that leisure time has a great number of positive factors. But not all leisure time is recreational or productive, and herein lies a degree of community tension.

To examine the buying habits of the American culture, it might seem that the increasing leisure of affluence has been dominated by recreation. Beginning in the decade of 1940–1950, expenditures for sports equipment or toys increased three times, musical instruments or sound equipment five times, and opera and legitimate theatre two times, opera companies increasing in numbers from two to thirteen.[1] The two decades that followed have shown the same trend. But not everyone has enjoyed the affluence implied by such data, and certainly not everyone has enjoyed affluence to the same degree.

One view of adversity is that it is more or less a "natural" consequence of "progress."[2] Of course, to accept such a viewpoint without challenge is to question the possibility (or at least to question the advisability) of programs geared to alleviate the adverse consequences of social change.

[1] F. Turck, "The American Explosion," *Scientific Monthly*, Sept., 1952, pp. 187–91.

[2] H. Meissner, ed., *Poverty in Affluent Society* (New York: Harper and Row, Publishers, 1966), p. 19.

But if community tension is to be reduced, the negative results of social changes that produce increased leisure must be conceived of as correctable. Correction, however, depends on a number of variables related to political and economic power.

Education

On a common sense basis, the demand for education increases in proportion to the social changes that result from advances in technical knowledge. With each discovery of new sources of energy and the development of machinery to replace human labor, a corresponding demand for increased sophistication in methods of productivity occurs. Automation, cybernetics, and EDP mechanization, on the one hand, close many avenues of employment by displacing employees. On the other hand, these factors create many new opportunities, but only for the well trained and educated. The access to and the significance of education then dramatically increases.

Before examining equality of access to education, some thought might be given the concept of social change as it relates to education in general. The occupational field of law enforcement itself serves as a model of the lag between social institutions and the rate of change in modern America. There are fewer police per 10,000 inhabitants in cities of growing population than in cities with decreasing population.[3] In like fashion, certain school programs for the "disadvantaged child" have lagged far behind the growth in the numbers of these children in the educational system.[4] This lag has continued in spite of the compulsory school attendance that distinguishes the United States from much of the world.[5]

Social change that brings increase in leisure also brings attention to education in two ways. As mentioned above, an increased demand for technical skill accompanies discovery of new sources of energy and labor-saving machinery. Here there is, of course, an obvious role for education and training.

[3] W. Ogburn, "Cultural Lag as Theory," *Sociology and Social Research*, Jan.-Feb., 1957, pp. 167–74. Also, *Social Characteristics of Cities: International City Managers Association*, 1937.

[4] R. Kerckhoff, "The Problem of the City School," *Journal of Marriage and the Family*, Vol. 26, No. 4, Nov., 1964, 435–39.

[5] E. Friedenberg, "An Ideology of School Withdrawal," *Community*, Vol. 35, No. 6, June, 1963, 492–500.

Social Change

But education draws attention to the *length of time* necessary to complete the education process.

Both family and public traditionally have been prepared to support the child's education through at least grade school and often through high school. But what about college? How much college?

Prior to what is often referred to as the "knowledge explosion, following the technical advances of World War II, college was not thought of as *essential* for many people. But automation, combined with government sponsorship through the "GI Bill" and other subsidized college programs, has rapidly focused attention on college training as a crucial part of the educational process.

To many, this social change has unveiled vast new horizons of opportunity. To many others, the social change has widened even further the gap between affluence and poverty.

For unlike the masses of middle-class families prepared and motivated to support children through the increasing expenses of education, poverty-stricken families necessarily consider the high school age child as a potential source of income, or at least as some relief from the drain on limited family income. The relatively restricted number of college students from poverty backgrounds should not then be surprising—even in the rare instances when *adequate* high school programs are available.

There are many sources of community tension, but none so great as the social changes that increase the disparity of potential to control one's destiny, and education is increasingly the prime ingredient of the potential of this control.

Community Tension

There are numerous "causes" of community unrest—many "causes" beyond the scope of law enforcement or of criminal justice. There is, nonetheless, a significant relationship between law enforcement and certain aspects of unrest. As noted earlier, symptoms of unrest frequently foreshadow direct intervention by law enforcement. Moreover, law enforcement may even become involved in various causal aspects of community tension. The relationship of law enforcement to community unrest has been placed in excellent context by Frank Remington's comments on arrest practice:

> ...from the point of view of either the individual or the community as a whole, the issue is not so much whether police are efficient, or whether the corrective system is effective, but whether the system of criminal justice in its entirety is sensible, fair, and consistent with the concepts of a democratic society. . . .[6]

In this context, at least part of community tension, as already noted, can be thought of as first a disparity between various citizens in terms of their potential to control their own destiny. Second, unrest may be thought of as a reaction to the method of enforcing conformity to a system that creates or permits this disparity.

In other words, a system that is "unsensible, unfair, or inconsistent with democratic concepts" may become as much a source of community tension as the social changes that created the original disparity in the potential to control one's own destiny.

Demonstrating Unrest Without Riots

Of course, determining what is "sensible, fair, and consistent with democratic concepts" may not be completely possible for law enforcement in an era of grossly divergent and constantly changing demands. But to the degree that law enforcement is able to achieve a sensible, fair, and consistent system, community tension is likely to be reduced.

The significance of reducing at least this area of community tension is probably most perceptible in terms of distinguishing between a "demonstration" and a riot.

Throughout this book this distinction is discussed as the *behavior* of the group involved. And more often than not, the behavior itself relates directly to law enforcement. It would seem reasonable to generalize that "rioters" rarely conceive of law enforcement as "sensible, fair, and consistent," or it may be that "demonstrators" do not riot simply

---

[6]W. LaFave, *Arrest* (Boston: Little, Brown and Company, 1965), Editor's Foreword.

Community Tension

because they believe the police have nothing to do with social changes that cause tension.

Obviously, this is not always true. There is overwhelming evidence that in many instances police have borne the brunt of violence erupting out of demonstrations against social problems clearly unrelated to law enforcement. But it remains a valid area of conjecture that at least the *degree* of violence relates to the attitude of the rioter toward law enforcement.

Regrettably, a system that is sensible, fair, and consistent with democratic concepts does not ensure a favorable attitude toward law enforcement.

Sensationalism

Elsewhere in this book, the psychology, sociology, and even the economics of prejudice, bias, and discrimination are dealt with as areas of concern for police in the changing community. Community-relations programming to be discussed in the concluding chapter and much of the "police image" already dealt with are related areas of concern. But in terms of attitudes toward police and their responsibilities in times of social change, another area of concern is the *sensationalizing* of problems and problem causes.

Sensationalizing problems and problem causes tends to aggravate community tension not so much through distortion of fact as through distortion of perspective. In the myriad contact of law enforcement with all segments of the public, some abuse of police power is real, some is fancy. Both are frequently reported. But at the heart of the problem of perspective is the newspaper adage that a dog biting a man is not news, but a man biting a dog is news.

Police are far more available and visible than any other "symbol" of government authority. But like the dog biting the man, police authority used to support an orderly society is expected and therefore of little news value. But, "police brutality," real or fancied, like man biting dog, is not expected and is therefore of great news appeal.

The "sensational news" of brutal policemen may serve two functions, both of which are relevant to the law enforcement struggle for a sensible, fair, and consistent system. First, sensational news is probably of higher commercial value.

Fig. 5.1 Law enforcement agencies are being confronted with problems over which they have no control. Demonstrations against the Vietnam War, strikes on campuses, and so on are some of the social problems causing tension in the community. Quite frequently, violence erupts out of demonstrations against a system that is considered—by those demonstrating—unfair or inconsistent with democratic concepts. Photo courtesy of the San Francisco Police Department.

Second, there is great attention-gaining value in sensationalism with any group seeking relief for real or even imagined social ills. Indeed, if there evolves a predictable acceleration of government social programming in areas of civil violence, then there may further evolve a motive for sensationally discrediting police in order to foster riot conditions.

As already noted, community tensions in large measure reflect social changes over which the police have no control. But the sensationalism of contact between police and the public is an area singularly susceptible to community-relations programming. And just as change is not always optional, the obvious methods of meeting the problems of change through awareness cannot be labeled unfeasible.

The manner in which all justice is dispensed, particularly in a changing community, must remain functional to be of value.[7] The response of law enforcement to social change in community tension must be functional or ultimately it is unacceptable. The weight of demonstrating the value of this function falls on law enforcement itself if gross civil disruption is to be avoided.

Change, particularly social change, is an ongoing process not subject to prevention but perhaps subject to influence. As the law-enforcing segment of Constitutional government strives to exert positive influence, it becomes incumbent on law enforcement to remain ever aware of the destructive potential of sensationalism.

[7]A. Coffey, "Correctional Probation: What Use to Society?" *Journal of the California Probation and Parole Association*, Vol. 5, No. 1, 1968, p. 28.

Social Change and Community Tension

Implications of Group Behavior for Law Enforcement

Built within the philosophy of our government are the concepts of freedom of speech and freedom of assembly. These freedoms create a special set of problems for the keepers of the peace; the practical implications for law enforcement regarding a citizenry that can assemble and peacefully demonstrate are quite great. Part of the problem lies in the fact that all citizens, from ghetto minorities to affluent college students, may demonstrate.

The sight of college students involved in politically-motivated mass public disorder is a rather new phenomena on the scene in the United States, although this type of behavior has been in evidence in many other countries over the years. The one difference between unruly mobs of college students and other unruly mobs is the emotional support that college students might be able to muster. The citizenry often tends to view college students as the flower of the nation's youth. Therefore, there might be a tendency to view police controls of these unruly college students as police brutality.

Another area of concern for law enforcement agencies is handling protests by the minorities of the ghetto. Police handling of these protests can make the difference between peaceful demonstration and violence. This is true because the members of minority groups often view police with a great deal of resentment and hostility. Therefore, any act which might be construed as imprudent could cause the hostility and resentment to erupt into violent behavior.

Another potential problem is in the handling of youthful exuberance. The exuberance that is found at teen-age dances or at high school athletic events, if uncontrolled or mismanaged by law enforcement agencies, can become a serious problem. Mismanaged, youthful exuberance can turn into youthful rebellion. This, in turn, may cause young people to lose confidence in authority.

chapter

6

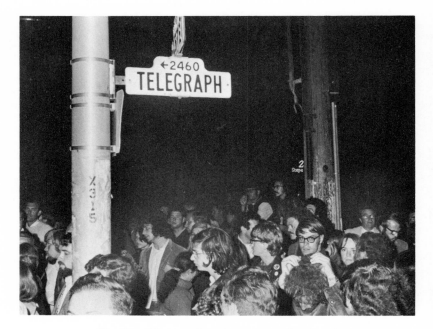

Fig. 6.1 When students become emotional and overreact to a political or social issue, it is incumbent upon law enforcement personnel to control this unruly mob (regardless of whether they are students) with whatever *legal* methods are at their disposal. Police officers must, however, be wary of overreaction to the situation. Photo courtesy of the San Francisco Police Department.

An investigation made by the President's Commission on Law Enforcement and the Administration of Criminal Justice indicated that one of the most frustrating tasks in police work today is controlling riot situations.[1] When a situation gets out of hand and develops into a civil disorder, it becomes a threat to the social order in a number of ways. These ways can be summed up as a threat to constituted authority, a threat to persons, and a threat to property.

Crowds

Civil disorder and violence or mob behavior historically has been interpreted in two ways. One has emphasized the

[1]*The Challenge of Crime in a Free Society*, pp. 118–19.

Implications of Group Behavior for Law Enforcement

group itself. This interpretation suggests that groups are more or less independent from the individuals who make up their composition. The other interpretation emphasizes the behavior of individuals who make up the group.

In the first interpretation of a crowd, it is felt that the individuals in the crowd are "swept up" and thereupon lose individuality. The crowd is considered uncivil and irrational. The participant, no matter how rational or civilized he might be as a person, is reduced to the beastial level.[2]

The second concept stresses the behavior of individuals acting as individuals with the recognition that individual behavior changes in certain respects in the presence of other people. In most instances, the presence of other people tends to have a restrictive effect on behavior. However, under certain circumstances, a permissiveness about a crowd situation may induce individuals to react in a less restricted way. An individual may not normally think of looting a store, but when others are looting he may join them. The thought that "everybody is doing it" and the feeling that he, as an individual cannot be singled out and punished for this act, may be responsible for this change in his behavior.

Crowd Types

According to H. Blumer, there are basically four types of crowds.[3]

The first type of crowd can be identified as a casual crowd. An example of this type would be a street crowd observing a display in a store window. The casual crowd has a momentary existence. It is very loosely organized, and the members of it come and go giving temporary attention to the object which has captured their interest. Their association with other members of the crowd is minimal.

A second type of crowd can be designated as a conventionalized crowd. An example of this would be the spectators at a football game. Their behavior is essentially the same as members of a casual crowd, except that it is expressed in established ways. An example of this is the football crowd's standing for each kickoff.

---

[2]G. Le Bon, *The Crowd: A Study of the Popular Mind* (New York: Viking Press, 1960).

[3]H. Blumer, "Collective Behavior" in A. M. Lee, ed., *Principles of Sociology* (New York: Barnes and Noble Inc., 1951), pp. 165–222.

Crowds

The third type can be called the expressive crowd. Excitement is expressed in physical movement, and this movement is a form of release; it is not directed at an object. This type of crowd is found in certain religious sects.

The fourth type of crowd is the so-called acting or aggressive crowd. The outstanding feature of this crowd is that it has an objective toward which activity is directed. This is a crowd that could easily be classified as a mob. It is this type of crowd that is most often of concern to police.

Characteristics of a Crowd

There are certain general characteristics which can be applied to all crowds:

Size: It is obvious that the very size of a crowd under certain circumstances may cause problems for the police. The thousands of people gathered at an athletic event may necessitate careful planning and organization, particularly regarding orderly movement. Police will probably be quite concerned with some plans for protection in case of an emergency caused by a disaster. However, generally speaking, the size of a crowd gives little indication about the nature and seriousness of any problems police may have to face, with the possible exception of traffic control. Police problems regarding a crowd are generally related to other characteristics. However, because ineffective handling of a crowd can cause problems, the size of a crowd may be an important dimension.

Dimension: Dimension refers to the length of time a group has been in existence. For example, a group or gang of boys may have been in existence a number of months before they congregate as a crowd on a street corner. Merely to chase the boys off the corner may disperse the crowd but in actuality bring more solidarity to this gang of boys. Social agencies such as police and juvenile probation may be more interested in steering this group into constructive goals rather than merely dispersing it so that it can become a healthy and useful group.

Identification: Whether or not a person thinks of himself as a member of a group and identifies with it is a consideration in the evaluation of a crowd. Identification is the process that occurs within an individual. Nevertheless, groups can be distinguished on the basis of the degree of the identification of the members. Identification may be known to other people. Other members of a group are frequently aware of one's membership in that group, especially if there is some kind of formal organization, congregation, or interpersonal communication. Strangers are often able to identify members of a group. An example is police who are readily identified by their uniforms.

Polarization: Another characteristic of the group is polarization. This occurs when members of a group focus their attention toward some object or event. A group may be polarized toward a speaker, a movie, or an athletic event.

A crowd may or may not be polarized. A group of passengers on a commuter train would probably not be polarized. They would be involved in individual pursuits, such as reading or talking. Suppose someone fired a gunshot into that commuter train car. At this point, in all probability, all the passengers in that car would be immediately polarized toward that event.[4]

The characteristics of a group were examined here because their manipulation by police can be very helpful in crowd control. Four examples of this might be:

1. Using "bull horns" to command the attention of the group is, in a sense, essentially an attempt to change the polarization (focus) of that group.
2. Taking photographs of the participants in a mob action often makes persons aware that they are members of a disapproved group. The protective anonymity of the group is lost, and identification with the crowd becomes associated with anxiety, causing the person to withdraw from the group.
3. Dispersing a crowd may terminate its duration physically.
4. Dividing a crowd into two smaller groups makes it easier to deal with.

[4]For further information about the characteristics of a group, see N. A. Watson, "Police and Group Behavior," N. A. Watson, ed., *Police and the Changing Community: Selected Readings* (Wash., D.C.: International Association of Chiefs of Police and New World Foundation, 1965), pp. 179–212.

Crowds

The Hostile Outbursts
of a Crowd

Many times hostile outbursts or mob actions follow a panic situation. A panic situation can occur when people feel trapped, when escape must be made quickly and the escape routes are closing. An example would be members of an audience rushing to the exits when they believe a theater is on fire and will burn quickly. In the panic situation, there is often strain from threat of physical danger. However, many strains are institutionalized. They may be due to differences in class, religion, political outlook, or race.

If hostilities are to arise from conditions of strain, these conditions must exist in a setting in which hostility is permitted or in which other responses to strain are prohibited, or both. An example would be in the handling of strained racial relations where hostility to members of a different race would be accepted by each race, and there would be no means to alleviate this strain such as by some type of discussion between the two racial groups.

Implications of Group Behavior for Law Enforcement

Adequate communication must be available for spreading hostility and for mobilizing for an attack. Individuals who do not understand one another and whose background or experience differ greatly are not easily molded into a mob. An audience, because it permits rapid communication, common definition of a situation, and face-to-face interaction, has many of the aspects necessary to become a mob. These aspects, simply stated, are: (1) strain, (2) the presence of a conducive setting, and (3) adequate communication.

With the spreading of truths, half-truths, and rumors through a group, the possibility that this information will become a generalized belief increases. If the group begins to believe the rumors and half-truths, then tension mounts and a hostile outburst may be easily provoked. The provocation is called a *precipitating cause*. A precipitating cause may justify or confirm existing general fears or hatreds. In racial outbursts, for example, the precipitating factor might be a report—true or false—that one of the other racial groups has committed some unwholesome or unsavory act.

Anticipating Violence

A police department needs to prepare long before violence occurs or even before tension appears. The good police executive will be assessing the possibility of outbreaks of violence and of nonviolent demonstrations long before they happen. He will be making plans and should be involved in the creation and development of a sound community-relations program. The signs of an approaching problem seem to follow a definite pattern. Tension rises rapidly, and responsible leaders on both sides of the question realize that this tension is building up and that it may erupt into violent disorder. Law enforcement officers will find more and more hatred directed toward them. Incidents involving the discontented group are expanded out of all proportion. This is true no matter what the ethnic composition of the group.

When tension is developing, law enforcement supervisory personnel need to make an earnest attempt to understand it. For if they fail to make a reasonably correct

Crowds

interpretation of the circumstances, the outcome could be disastrous for the community.

Gathering information about the rise of tension can be accomplished by requiring each law enforcement officer to report incidents which might be tension producing. Also, an effort should be made to obtain information about the development of tension from school teachers, social workers, and ministers, as well as from employees of the transportation industry. Finally, information from members of the business community, particularly tavern owners and liquor store operators, often can be most useful. This is because incidents reflecting tension often occur in public places of this sort.

Tensions caused by false beliefs founded on rumors and half-truths may be alleviated if social agencies can intercede. For this reason, among others, a great effort should be made to sustain a dialogue between dissident parties and the police. Through the discourse, police always have the opportunity of trying to correct half-truths and rumors by means of two-way communication. This should help to keep these rumors and half-truths from crystalizing into general beliefs.

In the event that a crowd becomes mobilized for action, it may be possible for police to forestall a hostile outburst by disrupting the organizational process or by removing leadership.

In the last analysis, when a hostile outburst occurs, the behavior of social agencies determines how quickly the situation is resolved. The manner in which force is exercised affects the encouragement or discouragement of further hostility. It has been shown that when authorities issue firm, unyielding, and unbiased decisions in short order, the hostile outburst tends to be dampened. However, when authorities are hesitant or biased, or when they actively support one side in a conflict, they tend to increase the expression of hostility. In quelling a disturbance, the best method is the impartial, neutral, firm use of authority.

Crowd Control

It is believed that when a group of people get together in a crowd they can be stimulated by the crowd itself to act in a manner beyond the limit of any action they would have taken alone. If this is the case, prevention of the gathering of a crowd may be in order. This kind of thing is often done in riot situations. This is done by declaring martial law or by imposing curfews and nonassembly restrictions.

In ghetto areas, riot situations have been touched off when police have made what originally appeared to be a routine arrest. Joseph Lohman has set forth some ideas about the handling of these kinds of situations:

1. The police officer must refrain from impulsive actions; therefore, he must ascertain the facts first.
2. Once the police officer has the facts, he should act quickly. A quick decision can anticipate and cut short the gathering of a crowd. A quick disposition of a matter tends to neutralize the consequences of such interracial hostilities when such emotions are present.
3. A police officer should continually try to emulate a "fair" and professional attitude. This type behavior commands the confidence and cooperation of the best elements in a gathering crowd.
4. If the persons involved in the original incident that the officer was called to investigate are excited and emotionally upset, efforts should be made to separate them from the crowd situation as soon as possible. Such a practice helps prevent communication of emotions and excitement to the more excitable spectators in the gathering crowd.
5. Generally speaking, indiscriminate mass arrests have a most undesirable effect on public attitude toward police. Mass arrests of this type invariably involve great numbers of innocent people. This magnifies the difficulty since the arrest of innocent bystanders creates the impression of excessive and unbridled use of authority, as well as incompetence.
6. When unruly crowds gather, it should be possible to mobilize an adequate number of police quickly. A show of force is preferable to a belated use of force. Once an incident gets beyond the control of the police, it can only be brought into control again with a great deal of difficulty; and the possibility of property damage is then quite high, coupled with the possibility of the loss of life. These situations should never be permitted to develop wherein control passes from the hands of the police authority to the crowd.[5]

[5]J. D. Lohman, *The Police and Minority Groups* (Chicago: Chicago Park District, 1947), pp. 102–7.

Crowds

Community Relations and
Group Behavior

The police are only one resource that may be used in trying to solve the problem of human relations and to relieve the consequences of crowd tension. Many times, police are accused of instigating or aggravating tension. These accusations are often untrue. However, they probably arise because the police are necessarily constantly involved in incidents involving public disorder. Police will be blamed for what they have done by a certain segment of the society, and they will be blamed for what they have not done by another segment of society. However, it is felt that police can do a great deal toward getting the cooperation of the responsible element in the community and, thereby, bring about adequate public support in crisis situations.

To get the cooperation of responsible persons in the community, the police must show responsible people potential problem situations. A police department is in an unusual position to know where and when tension could lead to the outcropping of crowd behavior. By making each patrolman report all incidents which have the potential of causing a crowd to gather, a picture of potential reaction can be obtained. Certainly, interracial group incidents should be reported. Incidents nearly always occur in public places. Therefore, as mentioned above, teachers, community workers, ministers, transportation employees, housing directors, and social workers will be able to add more information about these situations. Information of this sort can also be obtained from local businessmen, particularly poolroom operators and tavern owners. Because crowd situations are sometimes set in motion by the actions of juveniles, it is well to keep close tabs on juvenile gangs. Out of the predatory nature of some of the activities of the juvenile group, many serious incidents of friction have begun. Just the reporting of incidents by patrolmen will be of no value unless the information is assembled and proper steps are taken to alleviate tension caused by the incidents.

It would appear that one of the proper steps would be to enlist the cooperation of neighborhood leaders, particularly in ghetto areas. They should be included at the planning level, well before direct appeals during critical periods are needed.

Implications of Group Behavior for Law Enforcement

Such individuals might well be useful as an advisory group.

If confrontation between police and hostile crowds does take place after other attempts to resolve the situation have failed, then excessive use of force should be avoided. This means that just enough force to restrain an individual, if he needs restraining, should be used. It does not mean that a police department should hesitate to send adequate numbers of officers to try to help quell an incident. A large number of police responding to an incident may well be a *show of force* which is quite different from the *excessive use of force*. Generally speaking, there is no substitute for judicious and impartial acts by all police officers, but at the time of an incident tact may well be the ingredient which prevents that incident from getting out of hand.

The concern here with incidents that are potentially riot-producing in nature should not suggest that the role of the police agency in human relations is basically one of riot control. Rather, the role is essentially one of preventing such an occurrence, for the very foundations of government are involved in its success in minimizing internal strife. This means that the self-confidence and integrity of the police in guaranteeing public order are cornerstones of government. Riots cannot be tolerated by any nation. Once lawful procedures for the resolution of conflict and the redress of wrongs are violated or abandoned, the collapse of society is inevitable.[6]

[6]W. T. Gosselt, "Mobbism and Due Process," *Case and Comment: The Lawyers Magazine Since 1894*, July-August 1968, Vol. 74, pp. 3–6.

Attitudes, Prejudices, and Police Work

When people wish to describe how an individual sees a social situation and how he responds to this situation, they do so in terms of attitudes. An attitude can be defined as a way of seeing, acting, and feeling toward a person or object. Attitudes may be either negative or positive. Therefore, an individual could be favorably or unfavorably disposed toward a person or object.

Prejudice is included in this definition of attitude. Prejudice is an attitude that tends to categorize people or objects in a good or bad light without regard for the facts. In the United States, particularly, prejudice is thought of in connection with race.

To understand this better we should focus our attention on the general concept of attitude. Attitudes have five dimensions:

1. DIRECTION. What slant does the attitude take? For example, is it for or against the police?
2. DEGREE. How positive or negative is this attitude? Is it *extremely* positive or *barely* positive?
3. CONTENT. What is the reason for the attitude? Although different people may dislike police in the same degree, their attitudes are not necessarily the same. Investigation of the content of their attitude may show that they perceive the police in markedly different ways. One may dislike the police because of personal contact, while another may dislike the police because he has been taught to dislike police.
4. CONSISTENCY. How is the attitude integrated with and related to other attitudes that a person may hold? For example, one person may dislike police because he sees them as the enforcers for the power structure, while another person dislikes police, but this dislike does not fit into a general framework of beliefs and attitudes.

Internal consistency may well relate to the strength of the attitude which is discussed next.

5. STRENGTH. How long does an attitude persist? Some attitudes continue for a long time despite data that contradicts them. These would be known as strong attitudes. A weak attitude toward police, for example, might well be changed after a person has one good encounter with a police officer. On the other hand, a strong attitude, either positive or negative, toward police, probably would not be changed much by one encounter.

Negative Attitudes toward the Police

Generally speaking, minority group members and the black man in particular initially had their most important contact with white society through the white policeman. Therefore, the policeman personifies white authority. In the past, he not only enforced laws and regulations, but also the whole set of social customs associated with the concept of "white supremacy." Historically, law enforcement was on the side of the slavemaster against the slave. In more recent times, the so-called "Jim Crow" laws of separate facilities were stringently enforced by the police. Minor transgressions of caste etiquette were punished by the policeman on an extra-judicial basis.[1] This type of contact with the police has had its telling effect upon the black man's sub-culture and attitudes toward the police in the United States.

Most information shows that approximately two-thirds to three-fourths of the white community believe that police deserve more respect and are doing a good job, while approximately 50 percent of the black community feel police deserve more respect and are doing a good job.[2] These differences between whites' and blacks' attitudes regarding police range up to a 25 percent difference. Obviously, the Negro population has a much less favorable attitude toward police than does the Caucasian population.

[1] A. Rose, The Negro in America (Boston: The Beacon Press, 1948), pp. 170–88.

[2] Task Force Report: The Police, A Report by the President's Commission on Law Enforcement and Administration of Justice (Wash., D.C.: U.S. Government Printing Office, 1967), pp. 145–49.

Fig. 7.1 Surveys conducted by independent pollsters reveal that there is a great disagreement between Blacks and Whites regarding local law enforcement agencies.

The results of a survey first reported in the *Report of the National Advisory Commission on Civil Disorders*[3] indicate the different types of grievances which appear to have the greatest significance to the Negro community. Judgment with regard to severity of a particular grievance was assigned a rank. These judgments were based on the frequency with which a particular grievance was mentioned, the relative intensity with which it was discussed, reference to incidents that were examples of this grievance, and an estimate of the severity of grievance obtained from the person interviewed. The grievances were ranked by weight from one to four. Four points for the most severe, three points for the less severe, two points for third in severity, and one point for fourth in severity. Grievances were ranked in three levels of intensity. These three levels are shown in Table 3.

As can be seen, police practice is a grievance that ranks first. It was often one of the most serious complaints. Included in this category were complaints about physical or verbal abuse of black citizens by police officers, lack of adequate channels for a complaint against law enforcement,

[3]*Report of the National Advisory Commission on Civil Disorders* (Wash., D.C.: U.S. Government Printing Office, 1968), pp. 80–83 and 344–45.

Attitudes, Prejudices, and the Police

Table Three
Major Grievances Within Negro Communities

First Level of Intensity

1. Police practices
2. Unemployment and underemployment
3. Inadequate housing

Second Level of Intensity

4. Inadequate education
5. Poor recreation facilities and programs
6. Ineffectiveness of the political structure and grievance mechanisms

Third Level of Intensity

7. Disrespectful white attitudes
8. Discriminatory administration of justice
9. Inadequacy of federal programs
10. Inadequacy of municipal services
11. Discriminatory consumer and civil practices
12. Inadequate welfare programs

SOURCE: *Report of the National Advisory Commission on Civil Disorders,* p. 81.

discriminatory police employment and promotional practices for black officers, a general lack of respect for black people by police officers, as well as the failure of police departments to provide adequate protection to black people.

Some Suggestions for Changing Attitudes

A study conducted in Los Angeles by Robert L. Derbyshire,[4] shows another facet of attitudes toward police which may be quite useful to law enforcement in general.

The significance of this research for practicing policemen is not that it confirms the theory of many social scientists

[4]R. L. Derbyshire, "Children's Perceptions of the Police: A Comparative Study of Attitudes and Attitude Change," *The Journal of Criminal Law, Criminology and Police Science,* Vol. 59, No. 2, June 1968, 183–90.

that attitude is learned from cultures or sub-cultures, but rather that it proposes that attitudes can be changed with a little effort.

Changes in attitudes are brought about in various ways. Some ways involve the change in an individual situation. For example, a person might change his attitude toward police upon being sworn in as a policeman. Change in group membership may cause a shift in attitude. An example of this is the youngster who ceases to be a gang member and, consequently, improves his attitude toward police. Other changes in attitude are brought about through the impact of the persuasive effects of education. Broadly speaking, this means of changing attitude is one that each policeman can do something about. Nelson A. Watson stated the problem quite succinctly.[5] He indicated that every law enforcement officer should be aware that he is a symbolic threat to many people. He is regarded as a disciplinarian and often as someone to fear.

This fact, that many see a police officer as a threat, has some undesirable consequences. One of these consequences is the tendency to avoid the officer. Another consequence is the lack of cooperation by some people because they are reluctant to contact the police. Still another is the belief by certain people that the police are their enemies.

This is not to say that a policeman should not be regarded as a threat to law violators. However, if a law-abiding citizen regards him as a threat and a person to be avoided, this is not in the best interest of either law enforcement or the citizen.

Observation and experience have shown that there are many police officers who seem to have a knack for dealing effectively with almost everyone. They seem to have this knack because they have found a way to present themselves in a nonthreatening manner, or, at least, they seem to have found ways of minimizing the threat which their identity as policemen seems to represent.

The unfortunate facts are that on many occasions a situation develops into a police matter even though the police have no intention of having it become one. The reason this happens is that, often times, people expect it and police

[5]N. A. Watson, "Issues in Human Relations, Threats and Challenges," *Guides for Police Practices* (Wash., D.C.: International Association of Chiefs of Police), pp. 1–22.

Attitudes, Prejudices, and the Police

officers do nothing to offset this expectation. Individual officers can best try to offset this kind of expectation. Nelson A. Watson gives the following guidelines to help improve human relations skill, and consequently to improve attitudes toward police:

1. Don't be trapped into unprofessional conduct by a threat or challenge.
2. Make sure everything you do is calculated to enhance your reputation as a good officer—one who is firm, but fair and just.
3. When you are faced with a threat and can't tell how serious it is, try to "buy time" in which to size up the situation by engaging the person in conversation. Make a comment or ask a question to divert his attention, if possible.
4. Don't show hostility even if the other fellow does. Many times a quiet, calm, and reasonable manner will cause his hostility to evaporate or at least to simmer down. An important point is that the next time he will not be so hostile because he doesn't think you are.
5. Reduce your "threat" potential. Avoid a grim or expressionless continence. Be an approachable human being. Too many officers habitually appear gruff and forbidding.
6. Cultivate a pleasant, friendly manner when making nonadversary contacts. Be ready with a smile, a pleasant word, a humorous comment, when appropriate.
7. Let your general demeanor and especially your facial expression and tone of voice indicate that you respect the other person as a human being.
8. Let the other fellow know by your reception of him that you don't expect trouble from him and that you don't consider him a nuisance. (Maybe you do, but don't let it show.)
9. Show an interest in the other fellow's problem. Maybe you can't do anything about it, but often it is a great help just to be a good listener. Most people will respond in kind.
10. Go out of your way to contact people in the interest of improving police-community relations. Even though your department may have a unit which specializes in community relations, never forget that you are the real key to good police-community cooperation. No group of specialists can establish or build readily effective police-community relations without you. More impor-

Some Suggestions for Changing Attitudes

tant, however, is the *fact* that effective police-community relations means more to you than to anyone else. This means that you, more than anyone else, should be actively working toward the establishment or the improvement of police-community relations. The essence of good working relations between the people and the police is to be found in the way you handle yourself. You and your fellow officers on the street can do more to improve (and to destroy) police-community relations in one day than your specialized unit and your command staff can ever do.

11. There is an old show-business maxim that runs, "Always leave them laughing." Let us paraphrase that and say, "Always leave them satisfied." There are people who react to an arrest or a traffic ticket by feeling the officer was fair, was just doing his job, and they had it coming. They don't like it, but they have to admit that the officer did his job properly. When you render a service or react to a request, show some interest and give some explanation. This will promote good feelings which, if carried on consistently by the entire force, will have a cumulative effect, resulting in vastly improved human relations.

12. Try in every way you can to encourage people to work with the police for their own protection. Let the average citizen know that far from being a threat you are interested in being a help. Drive home the point that he is threatened by crime and disorder, not by the police.[6]

[6]Watson, "Issues in Human Relations, Threats and Challenges," pp. 21–22.

Attitudes, Prejudices, and the Police

Throughout history those finding themselves in the role of police have tended to think of their work in terms of either apprehending or in some other way dealing with criminals. Although the complexity of modern law has increased the proportion of individuals who may be technically labeled "criminal," the police tend to see their role as it relates to law violation—particularly police who define their duties as *law enforcement*. Certainly no valid criticism can be leveled at such a tendency. But in view of the preceding chapters in this volume, certainly there is indicated a substantial broadening of the police role to include not only control of crime, but influence over the disruptive tensions in the changing society as well.

Intergroup Attitudes
Versus Behavior

In Chapter Six, group behavior was isolated in terms of various phenomena relating to conduct. In Chapter Seven, attitude, as it relates to a number of significant variables in the police role in a changing society, was discussed.

In considering intergroup attitude as opposed to group behavior, a great deal of clarity is gained from the psychiatric observation: "community attitude studies do not necessarily tell us what people actually do."[1] If this is true in psychiatry, then it is certainly true in law enforcement: community attitude does not directly control the law-abiding behavior of people.

[1]M. Jones, *Social Psychiatry* (Springfield, Ill.: Charles C Thomas, Publisher, 1962), p. 32.

chapter

8

Rare is the criminal who does not respect at least some of the laws that he does not break. His attitude toward those laws that he does not break is possibly just as "law abiding" as the attitudes of noncriminal groups. Many embezzlers may identify with groups that are appalled at violent crimes. Perhaps many burglars maintain a similar group identity. Conversely, many assaulters and perhaps rioters may identify themselves with groups that consider the embezzler or burglar an unwholesome person. The income-tax cheater may well consider himself a member of a group maintaining a generally law-abiding attitude. The reward or "payoff" that presumably motivates the violation of one law may for any number of reasons not be rewarding in the violation of other laws. The violation of law, therefore, may not be motivated by "criminal attitude"—particularly if one's *general* attitude tends to correspond with that of a noncriminal group.

"Attitude," then, is certainly less significant than specific *behavior*—at least to law enforcement. But if attitudes are not specifically related to criminal behavior, then certainly there is a question raised regarding the relationship of attitude and intergroup behavior. And if attitudes in a community are not correlated with the kinds of behavior with which law enforcement must be concerned, a method is needed to anticipate at least some of the problems between groups before disruptive behavior occurs. And clearly this method must not be dependent on attitude or speculation about attitude.

Perhaps a brief discussion of the community segments forming "inter-groups" might prove valuable before considering prediction of the behaviors considered in the previous chapter. And perhaps some consideration of what the community *is* may be the starting point.

The Community

The discussion of "crowd types," in Chapter Six made a number of distinctions between composition and behavior. From this frame of reference, one acceptable definition of *community* might be "a human population living within a geographic area and carrying on a common, interdependent life."[2] But the depth and breadth of social problems discussed

2G. Lundbert, C. Schrag, and O. Larsen, *Sociology* (New York: Harper and Row, 1958), p. 128.

Community Relations and Human Relations

throughout this book could scarcely support the notion of a "human population" enjoying a "common, interdependent life." As a matter of fact, the notion that humans who live within a limited geographical area are just one population-group fails to gain support from discussion of the social problems in this book. But if the community has more than one population, and the law enforcement goal is a method of anticipating behavior that does not correspond to law-abiding attitude, then the first part of the method of achieving this goal must be the identity of each population.

But before a discussion of the identification of population groups or the anticipation of their behavior is undertaken, it should be emphasized that one goal of law enforcement is the reduction of stress between one population group and another. When no stress exists between populations, law enforcement can deal with other tensions or simply perform traditional police functions. However, when stress between populations does exist, law enforcement, in its efforts to anticipate disruptive behavior, becomes committed to reducing that stress (if for no other reason than as a primary responsibility to maintain an orderly environment). And the type of stress to be reduced, unlike the tension stemming from social change, is stress generated through intergroup and interracial friction. Of course, all sources of tension are inextricably interrelated, but friction between different populations in the community is of immediate concern to law enforcement.

The Multiple-Population Community

In addition to the types of crowds discussed in Chapter Six, another community classification exists—populations—that might be called any number of things, such as the public, group, mob, gang, etc. What the population is called, or the kind of group it is, becomes important because the "label" influences both the behavior of that population, and the response to it by other groups, including law enforcement. A population that gathers and calls itself, or is called, a "gang" may well behave in a way that is different from the behavior of a population labeled simply "the public." A great many differences are apparent in various groupings of people.

A population, then, may well never become a crowd or

Intergroup Attitudes Versus Behavior

Fig. 8.1 Black Panther demonstration. Usually such demonstrations are quite peaceful. But, nevertheless, because of their provocative stance, the organization is labeled a violent one and therefore objectively regarding their behavior during peaceful demonstrations is sometimes difficult. Photo courtesy of the San Francisco Police Department.

a mob simply because members of the population never "gather." But simply "gathering" does not necessarily create a mob or even a crowd. "Gathering" simply means being in close physical proximity; when a population "gathers," it customarily gains some label, but the behavior exhibited determines that label.[3] *Crowds* have been defined in terms of behavior. But crowds also could be defined in terms of "gathering," and in this sense, even the "mob" in certain instances could be equated with a crowd.[4]

But in order to move toward the kind of population to be considered in this chapter, the gang may provide some clarity inasmuch as the gang does more than gather regardless of the behavior after gathering. Unlike other groups, a gang is usually the same population each time it gathers. And it is this sameness that permits law enforcement to examine not

[3]Lundbert, Schrag, and Larsen, *Sociology*, pp. 382–85.
[4]K. Davis, *Human Society* (New York: The Macmillan Company, 1949), pp. 303–56.

Community Relations and Human Relations

only the behavior of the gang but the predictable and controllable influences on this behavior as well. The gang, like crowds and mobs, is a group—but a group with considerable continuing sameness.[5]

Sameness in a group on a continuing basis suggests still another term: *category*. The gang is a category because each member is a gang member, whereas each member of a crowd may or may not be a gang member. The category of gang member suggests a "sameness" in the group just as does the category of Anglo-Saxon, Negro, Puerto Rican, etc. But unlike the category of gang member, in the categories of Anglo-Saxon, Negro, or Puerto Rican there is no requirement of gathering. Categories then are the community population groups between which stresses may occur that forewarn of violence between community groups.

The Size of Community Populations

Among characteristics of a crowd discussed in Chapter Six was that of size. The size of a community population, or more specifically a category, refers, of course, to the number of persons in a group but it also refers to *proportion*—the size relative to the size of other population categories in the community. The population categories that outnumber other categories in the community might then be considered "majorities." Categories that are outnumbered by others, then, are "minorities." Stress and tension among these different size groups are the focus of this book.

Human Relations

The literature increasingly reflects a definition of human relations that implies avoiding police brutality.[6] A further definition includes police discretion or decision-making in

[5]J. Toro-Calder, C. Cedeno, and W. Reckless, "A Comparative Study of Puerto Rican Attitudes Toward the Legal System Dealing with Crime," *J. of Criminal Law, Criminology and Police Science*, Vol. 59, No. 4, Dec. 1968, pp. 536–41.

[6]See, for example, L. E. Berson, Case *Study of A Riot: The Philadelphia Story* (New York: Institute of Human Relations Press, 1966); C. Westly, "Vio-

terms of "police attitudes."[7] But since the concept of attitude has been dealt with in Chapter Seven, a more appropriate definition of human relations as applied to law enforcement might be: police participation in any activity that seeks law observance through respect rather than enforcement.

Regardless of how human relations might be defined, police interest in the subject should be related in some way to the behavior that threatens an orderly environment. Such behavior, it has already been noted, produces little agreement among behavioral scientists in terms of specific causes. Causes (such as alcoholism, poverty, broken homes, parental neglect) can be isolated which seem to turn one individual to behavior requiring police action, but do not dispose another person to behave in the same way—even though both are subjected to precisely the same "causes."

But whether or not behavioral science can agree on causes, law enforcement practitioners might well agree that there appears to be a relationship between at least certain kinds of behavior and certain kinds of community influences.

Before programs can be geared to alleviating unfortunate combinations of community influences and behaviors, a community's attitude toward police (or the police image) must be studied. This particular force, or influence, is of primary concern because the individual citizen who is convinced that police are brutal will probably find it difficult to respect police goals, regardless of how significant such goals are to the welfare of the community. And the validity of the belief may matter less than the strength of the belief about police: the individual usually functions on the basis of what is believed regardless of how true it is. The beliefs of individuals about police then are of primary concern in human-relations programming. Put another way, the confidence of the citizen is a goal of and a requirement for human-relations programs for law enforcement. Confidence, however, occasionally presents problems for law enforcement.

Unhappy is the police agency that functions in a community in which typical citizens "confidently" expect law

lence and the Police," *American Journal of Sociology*, Vol. 59, No. 34, 1953; *The Economist*, Dec. 31, 1955, p. 1159; E. H. Sutherlund and D. R. Cressy, *Principles of Criminology* (6th ed.) (Philadelphia: J. B. Lippincott Co., 1960), p. 341; D. R. Ralph, "Police Violence," *New Statesman*, Vol. 66, No. 102, 1963.

[7]J. H. Skolnick, *Justice Without Trial: Law Enforcement in Democratic Society* (New York: John Wiley & Sons, Inc., 1966).

enforcement to eliminate completely crime and safety problems—a totally unrealistic expectation. Another extreme is a community that expects absolutely nothing from law enforcement insofar as crime and safety are concerned and remains "confident" that nothing will be done.[8] Fortunately, goals for human-relations programs can usually fall somewhere between these two extremes, and the press is frequently instrumental in determining precisely where.

One of the more difficult tasks of any human relations programs in law enforcement is to "judge" public opinion accurately enough to determine what degree of public support police enjoy at any given time. In recent years there appears to have emerged considerable evidence that public support of law enforcement changes as rapidly in terms of "crime" as it does in terms of community unrest and civil disobedience.

Rather than produce answers, the attempt to judge public opinion will frequently raise still further questions as to whether the press and entertainment media *reflect* public opinion or *cause* it. This question is of particular concern to community-relations programs that can be evolved out of human-relations programs. When press coverage consistently headlines crime to the point of stimulating greater citizen discussion of police activities, there is an impression of higher crime rates—an impression that sometimes obscures the fact that communities less inclined to "sensationalize" crime may, indeed, have the highest crime rates. The press, of course, argues that the public is entitled to all possible information on crime and other social problems, and the ensuing compromises traditionally are resolved in favor of the press's point of view. Turning human-relations programs into meaningful community-relations programs requires the assignment of priority to the types of problems that are of most concern to the public.[9] Of course, any community-relations programs must take into account the long-range consequence of removing line officers from "nearly jelled" stakeouts, from patrols in "recently quieted" areas, from "barely adequate" traffic programs, and so on. The policy of "stripping" all services to satisfy a single and possibly a temporary need in no way

[8]O. H. Ibele, "Law Enforcement and the Permissive Society," *Police*, September-October 1965, p. 15.

[9]O. W. Wilson, "Police Authority in a Free Society," *Criminal Law, Criminology and Police Science*, Vol. 54, No. 2, June 1963, p. 175.

Intergroup Attitudes Versus Behavior

serves the community's long-range interest. And yet a crucial variable in community-relations programming is evidence that police are responsive to public opinion.

Community-Relations Programs

The community itself traditionally approaches problems, particularly social problems, through some kind of "council." Councils usually function to coordinate the activities of various groups or social agencies. A variety of opinions exists as to how involved the "coordinating" should become with broad community problems outside specific neighborhoods. But the central idea, nevertheless, is to bring the combined forces and influences of various agencies to bear on defined problems. In an era when a bad police image increasingly stimulates consideration of civilian police-review panels, law enforcement could scarcely ignore this obvious method of implementing community-relations programming as an extension of the human-relations efforts already discussed. And yet there appears to be something less than a conspicuous national trend toward police-community relations programs.

The overwhelming need for community-relations programming can readily be justified in terms of a possible "movement" toward civilian-review boards for all police, regardless of jurisdiction. An occasionally overlooked but equally compelling justification for community-relations programming rests in the sociological concept of *power*. To the degree that the police symbolize the power of a government to enforce rules there is a risk of unrest and discontent. Moreover, to that same degree must police seek to establish trust from those perceiving police power. Being unable to take citizen respect and contentment for granted, and further faced with a need to persuade at least part of the community that bad image is inappropriate, the police need effective community-relations programming.

Group Goals and Intergroup Relations

While the relationship of the "majority" to the "minority" is of vital concern, consideration of the majority alone is necessary before examining intergroup relationship in terms of potential stress—stress presumably proving to be the target of community-relations programming. With the obvious exception of "the ruling classes," minority groups down through history have had treatment far less favorable than have majority groups. There have been varying degrees of historical interest in "human rights" as pertaining to both the majority and minority categories. But in the treaties following World War II, this interest began to focus. The ruthless, wholesale slaughter of Jews, a minority group, by the Nazi regime no doubt motivated many of the demands for "human rights" that were voiced at the very first San Francisco meeting of the United Nations in 1945. But, ironically, the period since has been marked as having the greatest unrest America has ever witnessed between majority and minority groups.

Certainly there is little reason to believe that the United Nations "caused" unrest between groups. But it may well be that the same world-wide concern with individual dignity was the basis for both the initiative of the United Nations and the increasing militancy of various minority groups. Whether these factors are related or not, however, it appears that some American minority group members have done more to promote "human rights" than the United Nations itself. In the process, some of the behavior of certain members of the minorities involved may have increased the stress between majority and minority groups. Nevertheless, there can be little doubt that the period since World War II has been marked by a definite movement toward greater individual freedom and hopefully toward dignity as well—with or without intergroup stress.

The question then becomes: Why can't achievement of such a laudable goal as "human rights" serve as a positive "payoff" or reward? Why, indeed, it might be asked, should tension arise between groups in the community when all seek merely to control or influence their own destiny? Law enforcement must first understand tension between groups as the source of disruptive behavior (even when such behavior fails to correspond to the law-abiding attitude of the group) and must then conceive of such an understanding as the source of remedy to stresses and tensions.

Individual freedom of members of both minority population categories and the majority population categories is the implied goal of community-relations programming. In this regard, individual freedom is often said to "end at the end of the other fellow's nose." In terms of various population categories' having the mutual goal of individual freedom, the end of the other fellow's nose might instead be "the other category's dignity." That is, the individual cannot be free to strike the other fellow's nose, nor can any one population category be "free" to deprive the other population category of dignity—regardless of the proportional size of either.

It follows, then, that there must be restrictions on the goal of individual freedom in community-relations programming—at least if *dignity* is a part of the goal of freedom. The freedom to strike the other fellow's nose because he is smaller is not and cannot be dignified. Freedom to seek control over one's own destiny in the many diversified areas of education, economics, personal respect, and other considerations discussed throughout this volume, must of necessity remain *restricted freedom*—perhaps, as much freedom as is possible.

Community-relations programming, enriched with human relations efforts, recognizes that tension occurring between the majority category and minority category of populations is most often traceable to the failure of either or both groups to recognize the restrictions on their own freedoms—restrictions necessary to retain not only dignity but the orderly environment sought by all concerned.

Community-Relations Program Barriers

Earlier in American history various European immigrant groups were "the minorities" and, as such, suffered many of the disadvantages inflicted upon minority groups today. But unlike racial minority groups, European minorities have traditionally been encouraged to *expect* that a single generation "turn-over" would remove the language barrier—the characteristic that clearly marked them. European minorities were also encouraged to expect that one generation could do even more. In a single generation, the typical European minority group could reasonably expect that the majority category's clothing styles, living habits, and social skills would accompany the acquisition of a new language.

Being able to expect such dramatic loss of "minority identity" may well have motivated the incredible speed with which many immigrant groups undertook on their own the loss of minority identity—and did, in fact, lost this identity. Frequently enriched with occupational skills from "the old country," most Europeans have taken very few generations to join the majority. Were this possible in every instance, an "ideal" community-relations program would be to have one great majority, free of intergroup tension.

Many American minorities, however, are forever identifiable by racial characteristics. These minorities can never expect to "join" the majority category in the same sense as have minorities who were identifiable only by dress and language. Indeed, in many respects acquiring the social behavior, the dress, and the language habits of the majority category often tends to draw attention to the "minority stereotype."

Community-relations programs, then, must go far beyond acknowledging the racial minority despair that accompanies generation after generation witnessing a system of elevating nearly all minority categories to the virtual exclusion of certain minorities. To be meaningful, programs must be geared to the right of every man to be respected as a human being. Moreover, this respect flows from the belief that *all* humans are of the highest form of life, and that only their *behavior* can be called good or bad—bad behavior always subject to modification in proportion to the human dignity accorded.

The precarious path law enforcement must follow in determining when a community-relations program has too much "minority support" to appear valuable to the larger community (and vice versa) becomes more clearly marked and easier to follow when this distinction is made between the dignity of humanity and the ugliness of certain types of human behavior.

Annotated
References

AMOS, W., and C. WELLFORD, *Delinquency Prevention*. Englewood Cliffs, N.J.: Prentice-Hall, Inc., 1967. Chapters 9, 10, and 11 deal effectively with the relationship of economics, police, and the judicial process in the community.

BARNDT, J., *Why Black Power*. New York: Friendship Press, 1968. Identifies and isolates the positive value of political and economic power for minorities.

BERNE, E., *Games People Play*. New York: Grove Press, 1966. A candid, easy to read translation of modern psychiatric belief that even complicated human behavior is both meaningful and understandable.

BERSON, L. E., *Case Study of a Riot: The Philadelphia Story*. New York: Institute of Human Relations Press, 1966. A particularly good discussion of human dynamics involved in community tension.

BORDUA, D. J., ed., *The Police: Six Sociological Essays*. New York: John Wiley & Sons, Inc., 1967. Contains six essays by sociologists on the problems of the police work in a society in which freedom of the individual is a great concern.

CLARK, K., *Dark Ghetto—Dilemmas of Social Power*. New York: Harper and Row, Publishers, 1967. An exceptional coverage of the ghetto and the manifestations of social power.

DERBYSHIRE, R. L., "Children's Perceptions of Police: A Comparative Study of Attitude Change," *The Journal of Criminal Law, Criminology and Police Science*, Vol. 59, No. 2 (June 1968), 183–90. A report that leads one to the conclusion that negative attitudes toward police can be changed.

DRIMMER, M., ed., *Black History*. Garden City, N.Y.: Doubleday & Company, Inc., 1967; and BRONZ, S., *Roots of Negro Racial Consciousness*, New York: Libra Publications, 1964. Both valuable as contrast to the typical stereotype Negro background of American culture.

EARLE, H., *Police-Community Relations: Crisis in our Time.* Springfield, Ill.: Charles C Thomas, Publisher, 1967. An attempt to examine the complexity of problems confronting modern police in terms of the future role of community-relations programming.

ELDEFONSO, E., A. COFFEY, and R. GRACE, *Principles of Law Enforcement.* New York: John Wiley & Sons, Inc., 1968. Chapter 8 elaborates the direct police role in community relations within the framework of police organizational restrictions.

FORTAS, JUSTICE A., *Concerning Dissent and Civil Disobedience.* New York: The New American Library, Inc., 1968. A discussion of civil disobedience and the "right to dissent."

FREEMAN, W., *Society on Trial.* Springfield, Ill.: Charles C Thomas, Publisher, 1965. An exceptionally detailed review of modifications in modern judicial process.

GRIER, W., *Black Rage.* New York: Basic Books, Inc., Publishers, 1967; CLEAVER, E., *Soul on Ice*, New York: McGraw-Hill Book Company, 1968; COHEN, J., *Burn, Baby, Burn!* New York: E. P. Dutton & Co., Inc., 1967; CONOT, R., *Rivers of Blood.* New York: Bantam Books, 1964. Each volume contributes new dimension to the magnitude of social unrest.

HARLAN, L., *Separate and Unequal.* Univ. of North Carolina Press, 1968; CONANT, J., *Slums and Suburbs.* New York: McGraw-Hill Book Company, 1961. Both texts provide an excellent perception of the cultural institutions impinging on minority groups.

HARRINGTON, M., *The Other America: Poverty in the United States.* Baltimore, Md.: Penguin Books, 1963. An extensive and "hard hitting" coverage of the title subject.

HEAPS, W. A., *Riots, U.S.A., 1765–1965.* New York: The Seabury Press, 1966. Covers the history of some of the riots and civil disorders of the 200 years of this nation.

LA FAVE, W., *Arrest.* Boston: Little, Brown and Company, 1965. An extremely comprehensive coverage of the power-boundaries of law enforcement in the community.

LE BON, G., *The Crowd: A Study of the Popular Mind.* New York: Viking Press, 1960. One of the first serious treatises on crowd behavior and, therefore, of historical significance.

LOHMAN, J. D., *The Police and Minority Groups.* Chicago: Chicago Park District, 1947. Although this book is over twenty years old, it brings much to bear on the subject of civil disorder.

MARX, J., *Officer, Tell Your Story: A Guide to Police Public Relations.* Springfield, Ill.: Charles C Thomas, 1969. Deals with the attitudes and procedures of police agencies in the context of community-relations programming.

MAY, D., "The Disjointed Trio: Poverty, Politics, and Power," *National Conference on Social Welfare: Social Welfare Forum,* 1963, pp. 47–61. An excellent discussion of the relationship of power to poverty through the medium of politics.

MEISSNER, H., ed., *Poverty in Affluent Society.* New York: Harper & Row, Publishers, 1966. A collection of contributions dealing with the many influences of poverty and on poverty in the community.

MILLER, N. E., and J. DOLLAR, *Social Learning and Imitations.* New Haven and London: Yale University Press, 1941, pp. 218–34. The application of learning theory to crowd behavior.

MINUCHIN, S., B. MONTALVO, B. GUERNEY, B. ROSMAN, and F. SCHUMER, *Families of the Slums.* New York: Basic Books, Inc., Publishers, 1967. Excellent coverage of the title subject—particularly of corrective measures.

MOMBOISSE, R., *Community Relations and Riot Prevention.* Springfield, Ill.: Charles C Thomas, Publisher, 1969. The theme of this text is: *The only effective way to control a riot is to prevent it.* This theme is reviewed in the context of community-relations programming.

NOEL, D., "A Theory of the Origin of Ethnic Stratification," *Social Problems,* Vol. 16, No. 2, (Fall, 1968), 157–72. A plausible explanation of social separation of ethnic grouping.

NORDSKOG, J., E. McDONAGH, and M. VINCENT, eds., *Analyzing Social Problems.* New York: Dryden Press, 1950. A fine collection of contributions affording a classical analysis model for virtually all modern social problems.

President's Commission on Law Enforcement and Administration of Justice. *The Challenge of Crime in a*

Free Society. Wash. D.C.: U.S. Government Printing Office, 1967. The summary on pages v through xi gives an excellent context for the law enforcement role in the changing community. See also, the Task Force Reports from the same Commission entitled: *The Police* and *The Courts*.

Report of the National Advisory Commission on Civil Disorders. Wash., D.C.: U.S. Government Printing Office, 1968, p. 425. Because the Chairman of the Committee that was responsible for this study was Otto Kerner, this study is often referred to as the Kerner Report. This report is an extensive study of several of the more recent riots in the United States as well as an extensive investigation of the conditions within the ghetto. Particularly, attention is directed toward the conditions in the ghetto as they are related to civil disorders.

Rights in Conflict: The Walker Report of the National Commission on the Causes and Prevention of Violence. New York: Bantam Books, 1968. The investigation of the civil disorders and the police reaction surrounding the Democratic National Convention of 1968.

SKOLNICK, J., ed., *The Politics of Protest*, A Task Force Report—National Commission on the Causes and Prevention of Violence. New York: Simon and Schuster, Inc., 1969. A recent publication with a collection of contributions dealing with protest and politics.

SMELSER, N. J., *Theory of Collective Behavior*. New York: The Free Press, 1963, pp. 131–69 and 222–69. A discussion of the panic situation and of hostile outbursts as they relate to human behavior.

STEIN, H., and R. CLOWARD, *Social Perspectives on Behavior*. New York: The Free Press, 1967. A varied and comprehensive coverage of the nature of human conduct.

VAN DEN BERGHE, P., *Race and Racism: A Comparative Study*. New York: John Wiley & Sons, Inc., 1969. An excellent background for examining the cross-cultural ramifications of race relations.

WATSON, N. A., "Issues in Human Relations, Threats and Challenges," *Guides for Police Practices*. Wash., D.C.: International Association of Chiefs of Police, 1969, p. 22. Explains how police may inspire negative attitudes toward themselves. Twelve practical ways to strive for a positive police image are enumerated.

Annotated References

89

———, ed., *Police and the Changing Community: Selected Readings*. Wash., D.C.: International Association of Chiefs of Police, 1965. Covers every aspect of human and community relations. Very useful as a supplement to a text in police-community relations.

DATE			
MAR 17 '83